MARKETING PLANNING

A WORKBOOK FOR MARKETING MANAGERS

MARKETING PLANNING

A WORKBOOK FOR MARKETING MANAGERS

FIRST EDITION

Sally Dibb

Lyndon Simkin

SOUTH-WESTERN
CENGAGE Learning

Australia • Mexico • Singapore • Spain • United Kingdom • United States

SOUTH-WESTERN
CENGAGE Learning™

Marketing Planning
A Workbook for Marketing Managers
Sally Dibb and Lyndon Simkin

Publisher: Jennifer Pegg

Development Editor: Leandra Paoli

Production Editor: Alison Walters

Manufacturing Manager: Helen Mason

Marketing Manager: Angela Lewis

Typesetter: KW Global, India

Cover design: Nick Welch

Text design: Design Deluxe, Ltd, Bath, UK

For product information and technology assistance, contact **emea.info@cengage.com.**

For permission to use material from this text or product, and for permission queries, email **Clsuk.permissions@cengage.com**

Products and services that are referred to in this book may be either trademarks and/or registered trademarks of their respective owners. The publishers and author/s make no claim to these trademarks.

Cover photograph showing multi-coloured balls being released on a San Franciscan street for the Sony Bravia television advertisement © Bret Lama.

British Library Cataloguing-in-Publication Data
A catalogue record for this book is available from the British Library.

ISBN 13: 978-1-84480-782-6

Cengage Learning EMEA
High Holborn House, 50-51 Bedford Row
London WC1R 4LR

Cengage Learning products are represented in Canada by Nelson Education Ltd.

For your lifelong learning solutions, visit **www.cengage.co.uk**
Purchase e-books or e-chapters at: **http://estore.bized.co.uk**

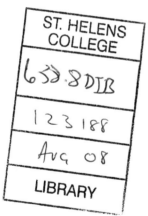
Printed by C & C Offset, China
1 2 3 4 5 6 7 8 9 10 – 10 09 08

Without marketing planning no company truly succeeds. In fact, without it, many companies fail to survive!

Marketing planning creates a focus on the customer, an awareness of competitors' strategies, and an understanding of market trends and challenges, so enabling effective use of an organization's resources and the development of carefully targeted sales and marketing programmes.

Strategies maximize opportunities and side-step principal threats. Marketing and sales programmes stress the company's advantages and convey a coherent message to targeted customers, dealers, partners and the marketplace.

Marketing planning as a process of analysis, thinking and action is essential for survival and long-term success. Marketing planning is not simply an academic exercise; it should become integral to a company's management style and ethos.

Without marketing planning, the organization will fail to take stock of the market's developments and will ignore emerging opportunities. There will be 'more of the same', with little likelihood of competitive advantage or market-facing innovation. Internal orientation to the core market drivers and challenges will be patchy and the organization is unlikely to have a transparent and appropriately aligned target market strategy.

Marketing planning is potentially hugely powerful and directional, but it is not without its difficulties. Most of these commonly encountered blockers can be pre-empted or speedily addressed, if the organization is proactive in seeking out problems.

Marketing Planning explains the essential activities of the marketing planning process, examines how to address the possible problems, and presents illustrative cases for how best to approach marketing planning.

This highly practical and applied book draws on the authors' 20 years of experience of researching and writing about marketing planning, and their extensive consultancy experience in this field.

For Rosalie Alice, Samantha, Mae, Abigail, James and Rebecca

BRIEF CONTENTS

CONTENTS

LIST OF FIGURES

PREFACE: THE RATIONALE FOR UNDERTAKING MARKETING PLANNING

Any business is an evolving organization: a collection of diverse units, talents and cultures in often fast-changing marketplaces. External pressures affect trading. Corporate goals demand more sales and higher profits. Life is busy and pressured for managers. Marketing planning really is able to help.

Marketing planning is a process conducted annually in most organizations in order to identify opportunities, understand challenges in the marketplace, prioritize target markets, specify appropriate marketing programmes, focus resources where they are most needed, and to instil a clear sense of direction for the organization. In this context, knowing the core issues to address and having a rigorous approach are fundamental requirements.

The process described in *Marketing Planning* has been tried and tested in a diversity of international and national organizations covering financial services and retailing, pharmaceuticals and chemicals, construction and engineering, telecommunications and IT, services and the not-for-profit sector, and even in government agencies. This process hinges on the *ASP* principle: first, (A) sound marketing Analyses to provide comprehensive and up-to-date marketing intelligence; second, (S) a pause to refine marketing Strategy by taking account of the revised analyses; and third, (P) the determination of detailed sales and marketing Programmes which incorporate the latest marketing intelligence and implement the determined target market strategies.

Marketing planning is not the sole domain of the Corporate Marketing Director, a business unit or the business development team. It is a *process* or philosophy which endeavours to raise awareness within the whole organization of the marketplace, trends, competitors and customer needs, to produce tight strategies and the means for their successful implementation, with optimum use of resources.

A customer focus is essential in today's trading environment. There are additional considerations, however. The dynamics of the market and government policy force a thorough understanding of general trends and market developments, along with more than a casual grasp of the activities of the organization's competitors, be they direct rivals or substitutes. Markets are often fast-moving: rarely is last year's marketing or business plan suitable for today's challenges or next year's threats and opportunities.

The core analyses within this marketing planning approach force an organization to consider in detail the needs and perceptions of customers (actual and potential), dealers and the sales force (where applicable), the media and policy makers. Competitors are monitored, their strategies predicted and their response to the organization's moves outlined. Market dynamics are assessed and the organization's successes and failures appreciated.

The most beneficial target markets are identified. Competitive advantages are maximized. The organization's sales and marketing programmes make the most of the company's strengths and resources. In addition, the programmes minimize weaknesses and tackle impending threats.

The cited benefits from marketing planning are significant, but the process of undertaking marketing planning and the operationalization of the resulting plan are not without problems. *Marketing Planning* presents a process for undertaking marketing planning successfully, but also addresses the most frequently encountered problems and blockers to progress. These insights facilitate effective marketing planning.

MARKETING PLANNING

This book has been prepared to lead managers through the marketing planning process: from the core analyses, into the development of strategies, and finally to the marketing programmes required to implement these strategies and take account of the core findings from the analyses. The process described adheres to accepted best practice and strives to deliver the full benefits possible from a robust marketing planning programme, as explored in Part One.

Each step is discussed in turn in Part Two, with explanation, guidance, step-by-step instructions and examples. Grids and charts have been produced for simple, quick, self-completion. The marketing plan finally produced will be concise, punchy and totally relevant to the organization's moves over the next three years and beyond, as explored in Part Three.

No matter how robust the adopted marketing planning process, there will be barriers to progress encountered. Most can be avoided, while those that occur as marketing planning progresses can be managed, as explored in Part Four. To illustrate the prescribed marketing planning process and the sorts of problems most commonly experienced, Part Five presents a set of real-world case studies.

Marketing Planning is in five parts:

- *Perspective to Marketing Planning*: an introduction to the marketing planning process and its benefits.

- *The Marketing Planning Process*: essential marketing analyses, from analysis to strategy, the creation of appropriate marketing programmes, operational controls and managing implementation. Step-by-step guidance for undertaking marketing planning.

- *The Marketing Plan*: explanation of the core components of a robust marketing plan.

- *Managing Marketing Planning*: awareness of probable problems and associated remedies.

- *Applied Illustrations – Case Studies*: learning from the experiences of a variety of organizations, including the service sector and SMEs.

Useful references and additional readings are listed at the end of this text.

Visit the *Marketing Planning* website at www.cengage.co.uk/dibb to find further valuable material.

Marketing planning plays a crucial role in helping an organization to maximize its potential opportunities and internal resources, take advantage of competitors' positions, target the most appropriate customers, and have a clear sense of direction. The approach presented in *Marketing Planning* and its supporting proformas has been deployed in many organizations to good effect. We wish you every success with *your* marketing planning.

Sally Dibb and Lyndon Simkin

ABOUT THE AUTHORS

Why take account of the authors' views and guidance?

They have researched and written extensively about marketing planning and target marketing for two decades, while teaching these topics to executives, MBAs and undergraduates at leading UK business schools. The authors have assisted numerous organizations in creating marketing planning processes, producing marketing plans or implementing resulting marketing plan recommendations. They co-chair the Academy of Marketing's Special Interest Group in Market Segmentation and have published many books and journal papers on the topic of marketing planning.

Dr Sally Dibb is currently Professor of Marketing at the innovative Open University Business School, having spent 18 years at Warwick Business School. **Dr Lyndon Simkin** is a Reader in Strategic Marketing at Warwick, one of the UK's leading business schools, and Academic Director of the IBM MBA. Sally and Lyndon have significant experience teaching undergraduates, MBAs and executives the basics of marketing, advanced strategic marketing, business planning, buyer behaviour, marketing communications and marketing research.

Sally and Lyndon's research focuses on strategy development, market segmentation, targeting strategies, marketing planning, business planning, strategy implementation and marketing modelling. They have published widely in these areas in European and North American academic journals. Their consultancy work has principally addressed business strategy creation, marketing planning and target market strategies in a host of UK and North American blue chip businesses, including AstraZeneca, the Audit Commission, Calor, Conoco Inc, Corus, Currys, Diageo, EDF Energy, Esso, Fujitsu, GfK, HSBC Bank, IBM, ICI, JCB, McDonald's Corporation, Nynas AB, PowerGen/E-on, Raytheon Inc, Royal & SunAlliance, Shell, Tesco, Tilda and corporate lawyers Clifford Chance and Freshfields, amongst others. Lyndon is an experienced expert witness in strategic marketing litigation court cases.

In addition to their joint authorship of *Marketing Planning*, Sally and Lyndon produce the market leading *Marketing: Concepts and Strategies* (Boston: Houghton Mifflin, now in its fifth edition with sales of over 400 000 copies) with US marketing colleagues Bill Pride and OC Ferrell, as well as the practitioner-oriented *The Market Segmentation Workbook* and *The Marketing Planning Workbook* (both London: Thomson), which help marketing managers to re-assess their target markets and understand the complexities of marketing planning. Sally and Lyndon also author the popular student revision aid *Marketing*

Briefs (Oxford: Butterworth-Heinemann) and *The Marketing Casebook: Cases and Concepts* (London: Thomson). Their latest book is *Market Segmentation Success: Making It Happen!* (New York: Haworth).

Readers who enjoy the format of this workbook should note that *Market Segmentation Success: Making It Happen!* offers a similar style of applied guidance for the creation of market segments and a target market strategy.

ACKNOWLEDGEMENTS

Many individuals and organizations have contributed to the ideas within *Marketing Planning*. Mention must be made of Anne, Ian, Peter, David, Dominic and colleagues from Fujitsu; George at CapGemini; Lesley, Rohit, Shilen, Umesh, Stephen, Ping, Vijay, Tony and colleagues at Tilda; Stuart, St John and colleagues at EDF Energy; Anette and Norbert at GfK in Germany; John at AstraZeneca; Ken at T-Systems; Adam at Eat Big Fish; Peter at Adsearch; Jim, Steve, Andrew, Kevin, Richard, David and colleagues at Raytheon; Fuad and colleagues at Azercell; Eka, Irina and colleagues at Geocell; Russell and fellow Directors at Box Technologies; James and Philip at St Andrew's Health-care; Anne and Mark at Willis; The ICI Market Focus Bureau; and David at QinetiQ, amongst others. Their enthusiasm for marketing planning and marketing strategy nurtured the sentiments within this book. A special mention must go to John Bradley, formerly of JCB and co-author of our first book about marketing planning. We remain indebted for our interest in all things marketing to former colleagues Peter Doyle, John Saunders and Robin Wensley.

More than anyone, our thanks go to Rosalie, Samantha, Mae, Abby, James and Becky – six wonderful children who motivate us and keep us sane!

LIST OF REVIEWERS

Haydn Blackey, University of Glamorgan
Chris Chapleo, University of Portsmouth
Fiona Davies, Cardiff University
Patrick De Pelsmacker, University of Antwerp
Dayananda Palihawadana, University of Leeds

PART ONE

PERSPECTIVE TO MARKETING PLANNING

Part One of *Marketing Planning* outlines the nature of marketing planning, its role in an organization and the process required to produce sound, realistic and effective marketing plans. There is also a comparison of this book's approach with other popular marketing planning schemes.

- Marketing planning defined.

- The importance of marketing planning.

- The marketing planning process.

- How authors view the marketing planning process.

1

Marketing planning

Marketing planning is an approach adopted by most successful market-focused organizations. While it is not a new tool, evidence suggests it is still undertaken to varying levels of objectivity and thoroughness. This workbook presents a straightforward format for conducting comprehensive market analyses, making the most of the resulting marketing intelligence to determine marketing strategies, and for ensuring detailed, actionable marketing programmes are put in place which implement the recommended strategies. Successful implementation of the marketing plan is the ultimate objective of a marketing planning initiative. Before the 'how to do' guidance for effective marketing planning provided in Parts Two to Five, *Marketing Planning* commences with a brief overview of marketing planning, its process and its benefits. This chapter aims to:

- define marketing planning and appreciate its benefits;
- introduce approaches to undertaking marketing planning;
- look at links between how different authors view marketing planning;
- examine the marketing planning process.

1.1 DEFINITIONS

The *marketing concept* holds that the key to achieving organizational goals lies in determining the needs and wants of target markets, and delivering the desired 'satisfaction' more effectively and efficiently than competitors.

According to the American Marketing Association, *marketing* is defined as both an organizational function and a set of processes for creating, communicating and delivering value to customers and for managing customer relationships in ways that benefit the organization and its stakeholders.

Marketing planning is a systematic process involving assessing marketing opportunities and capabilities, determining marketing objectives, agreeing target market and brand positioning strategies, seeking competitive advantage, creating marketing programmes, allocating resources and developing a plan for implementation and control.

The *marketing plan* is the written document or blueprint for implementing and controlling an organization's marketing activities related to a particular marketing strategy.

An organization's marketing *opportunity* is an attractive arena for sales and marketing activity, in which the organization might enjoy competitive advantage and effectively leverage its capabilities.

1.2 WHY CONDUCT MARKETING PLANNING?

Formal marketing planning is not a whim of textbooks or a few marketing directors. It is a recognized, widely-used approach by most successful, market-focused, customer-orientated organizations. From BP, CapGemini, Chester Zoo, Dell, Disney, Electrolux, Fujitsu, Heineken, Masterfoods, Nike, Royal and SunAlliance, St Andrew's Healthcare, Tesco and Unilever to government agencies and not-for-profit organizations, marketing planning keeps companies in-tune with trends in the marketplace, abreast of customer needs and often ahead of the competition. Their marketing planning utilizes resources effectively, minimizes the unexpected or avoids crises, while aligning executives to an agreed set of objectives and actions.

- Marketing planning hinges on core analyses of trends, customers, competition and capabilities.
- Planning develops strategies which target the best, most rewarding customers.
- Resulting strategies concentrate on the organization's real and perceived advantages in its markets.
- Action programmes – marketing mixes – help to ensure the implementation of these strategies.
- Resources concentrate on achieving these plans.

Some companies operate three- or five-yearly planning cycles; some every six months. Most opt for an annual revision with a three-year focus. In this way, the marketing plan includes detailed recommendations for the next two years, with extrapolations for the third year. The detailed analyses and plans are then updated annually.

Marketing planning is about:

- hitting the *best* customer targets;
- winning new customers;
- expanding markets;
- beating the competition;
- keeping abreast of market developments;
- maximizing returns;
- using resources to best advantage;
- minimizing threats;
- identifying company strengths or weaknesses;
- aligning an organization around shared objectives and planned actions;
- enhancing performance.

Without marketing planning, it is difficult to guide research and development (R&D) and new product development (NPD); reflect evolving market conditions; remedy weaknesses; set required standards for suppliers; guide the sales force in terms of what to emphasize, to whom and what/whom to avoid; set realistic, achievable sales targets; avoid competitor actions or changes in the marketplace. Above all, without marketing planning, marketing strategy is less likely to be updated or fully reflected in the organization's sales and marketing activities, and resources will not be realigned to reflect the most desirable opportunities.

1.3 THE MARKETING PLANNING APPROACH

There is a logical approach to marketing planning:

(a) Consideration of the organization's mission statement/corporate goals.
(b) Analysis of markets and the trading environment.
(c) Determination of priority opportunities, core markets and targeting strategy.
(d) Identification of a differential advantage or strengths to leverage.
(e) Statement of goals, desired product/service positioning and performance measures.
(f) Development of marketing programmes to implement plans.
(g) Allocation of resources and the creation of management controls.

The analysis of target markets, existing and new competitors – direct and indirect – and of the marketing environment creates a firm foundation for decision making. Without an understanding of customer segments, trends and competitors, the marketing programme is based on no clear strategy.

The marketer must strive to determine a basis for competing or a competitive edge in each of the targeted market segments. The selection of target markets and the determination of a differential advantage must take into account the organization's capabilities, and its strengths and weaknesses. The determined strategy should also relate to the organization's mission statement or sense of purpose.

To implement the planned strategy, a marketing programme must be formulated which – through the elements of the marketing mix – takes the product, service or expertise to the targeted customers in the most beneficial and clear manner.

The costs associated with implementing this marketing programme must be calculated and justified with accurate sales forecasts as part of the marketing plan.

1.4 THE MARKETING PLANNING PROCESS

As outlined in Figure 1.1, there is a three stage process for marketing planning: the *ASP* Model: Analysis, Strategy, Programmes, or information, thinking and implementation.

Each of these ingredients of marketing planning is explored in Part Two of *Marketing Planning*, which explains how to undertake marketing planning, step-by-step, from marketing analyses to marketing strategy decisions to marketing programmes. Part Three explains the content of the marketing plan.

1.5 HOW OTHER AUTHORS VIEW MARKETING PLANNING

Many books and papers have been published which describe the principles and process of marketing planning. Authors writing on the topic sometimes differ in how they present the process: some may use different jargon, describe the stages in different ways, or choose to place greater or lesser emphasis on certain elements. Even so, there is remarkable consistency in terms of the basic components which are described. The *SOSTAC* acronym (created in 1983 by P. R. Smith: www.PRSmith.org) is one such example, describing the following planning stages: *Situation analysis*, *Objectives*, *Strategy*, *Tactics*, *Action* and *Control*. Malcolm McDonald's (2007) marketing planning stages cover similar ground, comprising: Goal setting (mission and corporate objectives); Situation review (marketing audit, SWOT, assumptions); Strategy formulation (marketing objectives and strategies, estimates, alternative plans and mixes); Resource allocation and monitoring (budget, first year implementation programme, measurement and review).

FIGURE 1.1   The *ASP* approach to marketing planning

1. ANALYSIS

- Analysis of existing performance and the product/brand portfolio
- Analysis of the marketing environment, market trends and market drivers
- Analysis of competition, competitors' strategies and brand positionings
- Analysis of the organization's Strengths, Weaknesses, Opportunities and Threats – SWOT
- Analysis of customers' needs, buying behaviour, perceptions, and market segmentation

2. STRATEGY DECISIONS

- Selection of opportunities to pursue
- Determination of core target markets
- Identification of the basis for competing/differential advantage
- Choice of the desired product/brand positioning
- Agreement of marketing objectives

3. PROGRAMMES AND CONTROLS FOR IMPLEMENTATION

- Specification of sales targets and expected results
- Creation of appropriate marketing mix programmes:

  - Products
  - Promotion/Marcoms
  - Distribution/Channels
  - People/Service levels
  - Pricing/Payment terms

- Specification of tasks, responsibilities, timing, costs and budgets
- Internal communication and coordination
- Ongoing marketing research and performance monitoring
- Resourcing strategies

FIGURE 1.2 A comparison of marketing planning approaches: SOSTAC, McDonald and ASP

SOSTAC	McDonald's four phases	ASP process	Linkages and connections
SITUATION ANALYSIS Assessment of 'where we are now?', what is going on in the market, what are competitors doing, what are the key trends?	**PHASE 1: GOAL SETTING** Mission Corporate objectives	**ANALYSIS** Review performance and current portfolio Marketing environment, Competition analysis SWOT analysis Customer analysis	All three approaches commence with an analysis of the situation. There are small but insignificant differences in the relative emphasis. McDonald explicitly reviews corporate mission and objectives. These elements are implicit in the other approaches.
OBJECTIVES Details of 'where are we going?' or 'where do we want to be', described quantitatively	**PHASE 2: SITUATION REVIEW** Marketing audit SWOT analysis Assumptions		
STRATEGY Discussion of 'how do we get there?', summarizing how objectives will be fulfilled: which segments and propositions will be used	**PHASE 3: FORMULATE STRATEGY** Marketing objectives and strategies Estimates of expected results Identification of plans and mixes	**STRATEGY** Select opportunities Determine core target markets Identification of differential advantage Choose product/brand positioning Agree marketing objectives	The next elements relate to strategy development and objective setting. While the order in which these are handled varies slightly, the content is broadly the same in each approach. The degree of detail specified in the marketing mixes varies at this stage, but this is resolved by the end of the subsequent stage.
TACTICS Details of strategy, explaining how the strategy will be implemented		**PROGRAMMES** Set sales targets and expected results Create marketing programmes: Specify responsibilities, timing, costs and budgets Internal communication Performance monitoring Resourcing strategies	Detailed issues of implementation are now considered. SOSTAC and ASP first scope out the broad approach before fine-tuning the implementation plans. McDonald has already identified broad plans which are now described in more detail. All approaches then consider performance monitoring approaches. ASP explores future resourcing.
ACTION Detailed marketing programme tactics	**PHASE 4: RESOURCE ALLOCATION AND MONITORING** Budget Year 1 implementation programme		
CONTROL Systems to measure/monitor success			

Sources: SOSTAC, created 1983 by P. R. Smith: www.PRSmith.org; M. McDonald, (2007), *Marketing Plans: How to Prepare Them, How to Use Them*; Elsevier Butterworth Heinemann: Oxford; ASP, S. Dibb, L. Simkin, O. C. Ferrell and W. Pride (2006), *Marketing: Concepts and Strategies*, Houghton Mifflin: Boston. Used with permission; S. Dibb and L. Simkin (1996), *The Marketing Planning Workbook*, Thomson: London.

The parallels between the *ASP* process and the work of these high profile marketing planning writers are aptly illustrated in Figure 1.2. Reviewing this illustration will help readers to make connections between the information presented in this book and what they might read elsewhere.

1.6 THE MARKETING PLANNING CYCLE

As depicted in Figure 1.3, marketing planning never ceases: it is an on-going analysis/planning/control process or cycle. Many organizations update their marketing plans annually, presenting the key recommendations to all senior managers. Markets do not stand still, so neither can marketing plans. However, the workload reduces year-on-year, as updating requires less input. The *heartache* comes with the initiation of marketing planning during the first year of thoroughly undertaking marketing planning! It is easier in subsequent years. After three cycles or seasons, those involved often remark that marketing planning has

FIGURE 1.3   The marketing planning cycle

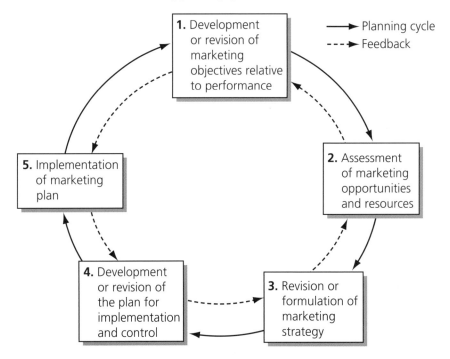

Source: S. Dibb, L. Simkin, O. C. Ferrell and W. Pride, *Marketing: Concepts and Strategies*, Fifth edition. Copyright © 2006 Houghton Mifflin Company. Used with permission.

become 'second nature' and that the necessary analyses are being routinely updated throughout the year whenever opportunities occur to consider market drivers, competitors and customers.

SUMMARY

Marketing planning is an effective tool for understanding the mechanics of target markets and for formalizing an organization's sense of purpose. Having completed essential background marketing analyses, the marketing team should be in a position to determine its key strategic direction: which are its priority target markets, what is the desired brand positioning in each market, where does the organization benefit from any advantage over competitors and what are the core marketing objectives? The detail of the resulting marketing plan focuses on the specified marketing action programmes required to implement these strategic requirements, making the most of identified marketing opportunities with the optimum use of personnel, time and budgets. *Marketing Planning* continues with a thorough review of each of these *ASP* steps, commencing with an examination of the required marketing analyses.

PART TWO

THE MARKETING PLANNING PROCESS

Step-by-step guidance for undertaking marketing planning. Part Two examines the process for marketing planning, commencing with the required marketing analyses, before considering the marketing strategy aspects of marketing planning and then the marketing programmes at the heart of a robust marketing plan.

The success of marketing planning depends on developing a clear understanding of the marketplace and trends, while appreciating the organization's capabilities. In order to agree a realistic target market strategy, it is necessary to analyse customers' needs, buying behaviour and their perceptions of competing propositions. It is essential to assess competitors' capabilities and strategies. Core marketing analyses are required in order to consolidate adequate marketing intelligence with which to make strategic decisions. Part Two of *Marketing Planning* first outlines the information required, including proforma templates for ease of assimilation.

Based on topical marketing analyses, the next phase of marketing planning updates the organization's marketing strategy. With the strategy devised and agreed, appropriate marketing programmes are formulated, costed and rolled out. Effective execution of these marketing programmes is a necessity for successful marketing planning and the implementation of the resulting marketing plan. This Part of *Marketing Planning* also examines these phases of the marketing planning process.

- Analysis of current performance, market trends and the marketing environment, customers, competitors, the portfolio and perceptions of these products or services, plus SWOT considerations of strengths, weaknesses, opportunities, threats.

- Corporate aims, opportunities to pursue and target markets/ segments, competitive advantage, brand positioning, marketing objectives and the requirements for marketing programmes.

- Detailed actions – marketing programmes – required to implement target market strategies and the marketing plan; allocation of responsibilities, resources, budgets and schedules; ramifications for other areas of the business and on-going work requirements; performance measurement and assessment of progress.

2

Existing markets/sectors

In any organization, the start of the marketing planning process must be the examination of the existing mix of customers, their worth to the organization and an assessment of current performance. Few organizations can ignore existing operations and market structures during planning. Much of the current thinking and previously agreed marketing actions will be worthy of incorporating into the newly developed marketing plan.

The existing view of customer segments and primary sales targets will be based on a mix of common sense and historical information about the market and individual customers. Much, but not all, of this information will be valid, up-to-date and useful. The organization's systems and structures, particularly in the context of sales priorities and the sales force, may well be carefully thought through and of merit. However, in most organizations, 'historical perceptions' of who or what the priorities have been in the past, tend to cloud judgement regarding current customer targeting and sales forecasting. With the pace of change of customer needs and the volatility of markets in terms of competition and market trends, there is always a need to re-examine targets.

This chapter will:

- provide a basis for marketing planning by appreciating current performance and the relative importance of different customer groups;
- assess points of weak performance;
- identify areas fundamental to the organization's trading and future growth.

2.1 APPROACHES TO THE ANALYSIS

There are four key stages to re-examining the existing customer base, priorities and segments. These involve considering who are the customers and what they are worth:

(i) State how customers are currently broken down into sub-groups or segments by the organization. For example, in business-to-business or industrial markets, is this done by customers' industry sector; their customer type; their purchasing patterns (seasonal, regular, etc.); the types of products purchased; territory, or some other criteria? In consumer markets, the organization may have determined segments by sales patterns, social class, age, sex, lifestyle, buying patterns, retail orientation, etc. No matter what criteria are used, it is helpful to consider whether such categorizations are commonplace within the particular industry.

(ii) For each existing segment or identified group of customers, summarize *their* product, dealer, sales and marketing needs, which the organization must be able to satisfy. In other words, consider the nature of the Key Customer Values (KCVs): the principal sales, product and marketing aspects valued or demanded by customers and perhaps offered by competitors.

Steps (i) and (ii) can be summarized in just one table, as illustrated in Figure 2.1.

FIGURE 2.1 Summary of existing target markets/segments

Existing customer group, target market or market segment label	These customers' key needs (KCVs)	Adopted descriptions used by the organization to describe the target market/ market segment
1		
2		
3		
4		
5		
6		
7		
8		

- Rank target markets/market segments in column 1 in order of importance (performance) to the organization
- For each market/customer group/market segment, rank the KCVs listed in column 2 in order of importance to these business customers or consumers
- Define the key customer value (KCV) term if required so as to avoid any ambiguity

(iii) It is likely that the composition of these markets has changed over time, and the importance of each market to the organization has altered. Tabulate for the past six to ten years the rank order of importance of these markets to the organization, adding explanatory footnotes where the running order alters significantly (e.g. if a market ranked 2 in 1999 is only ranked 9 in 2008). See Figure 2.2.

(iv) Summarizing these year on year moves should have set a few alarm bells ringing. Why is so much importance placed on market 'X'? Why is the sales force still devoting so much resource to market 'Y'? What about market 'A' – suddenly it seems more important? Is it?

The final stage in examining the recent history of the organization is to evaluate the financial worth of these markets – and major individual customers – to the organization. The Financial Director's involvement is invaluable. The most common approach is to examine sales and

FIGURE 2.2   Changing importance of priority markets

Rank order of markets by year										
Target market or segment	**1999**	**2000**	**2001**	**2002**	**2003**	**2004**	**2005**	**2006**	**2007**	**2008**
1										
2										
3										
4										
5										
6										
7										
8										
Reasons for major changes										

- Rank each market's/segment's importance over the years. Importance may be in terms of sales volumes, market share, profitability or contributions
- Explain any major changes in rank position year on year

contribution (the financial value to the company) in an ABC Pareto Analysis.

2.2 THE ABC SALES: CONTRIBUTION ANALYSIS

2.2.1 For market segments or territories

Data
List out, market by market, current sales in either volume or turnover. Turnover (e.g.: £s, $s or euros) is more common. List out, segment by segment, current levels of financial contribution (sales revenue minus all variable costs).

Graph
On a standard, two-dimensional (X-axis and Y-axis) graph, plot out sales and contributions. Log scales may be appropriate subject to data ranges.

- Y-axis (vertical): sales.
- X-axis (horizontal): contribution.

Evaluation
In an ideal world, the dots on the graph (each dot represents a market, customer group or segment) would be located in the top right segment of the graph: high sales and high contribution. Or, 'sell a lot, make a lot' ('A' class). Typically, however, this is not the case. The majority of markets fall into the bottom left segment of the graph (low sales and low contribution: 'C' class segments), or they have reasonably high sales, but low contributions ('B' class).

Diagnosis
Not all of the plotted markets will be close to the 45 degree diagonal line optimum. In almost all cases there will be outliers requiring attention. A question mark should hang over any market/product located in the bottom left segment of the graph: these products or markets are draining sales and marketing resources, without offering any obvious return to the organization. It is important to question whether there is any benefit in continuing to service these markets. Is a presence needed to protect the organization's other markets and products from competitive in-roads? Would other customers worry if the organization pulled away from these low-benefit customers? Are there seasonal reasons for this currently poor return? If the answers are 'no', new targets may be required.

FIGURE 2.3   Example of ABC sales: contribution chart

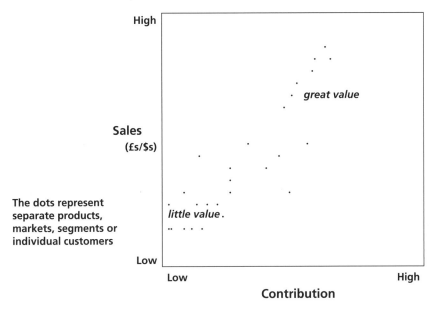

Can improvements be made? High volume markets to the upper left of the 45 degree line, with low contributions, would be of tremendous value if contributions were increased by only a few percent. Similarly, high contribution markets where current volumes are low (those plotted to the lower right of the 45 degree line) are crucial targets: even a minor increase in sales volumes should be very lucrative to the organization.

Clearly such 'movements' and improvements are not always possible. For markets in the bottom left area of the graph, harsh decisions may be required, as these markets seem to be of little value to the company.

2.2.2 For individual customer accounts

So far this ABC sales: contribution has concentrated on the market (segment) level. The completed analysis may well show a whole market to have relatively little value for the business. The second level of analysis is to examine individual key customer accounts in a similar manner. This analysis can be by either Product or Product Mix.

Data
List out, customer by customer, current sales in either volume or turnover. Turnover (e.g.: £s, $s or euros) is more common. List out, customer by customer, current levels of financial contribution (sales revenues minus all variable costs).

Graph

On a standard, two-dimensional (X-axis and Y-axis) graph, plot out sales and contributions. Log scales may be required owing to data ranges.

- Y-axis (vertical): sales.
- X-axis (horizontal): contribution.

Evaluation and diagnosis

The final two stages, evaluation and diagnosis, are the same as the approach for assessing whole markets or segments. The ease of dropping customers of little value (those in the bottom left portion of the graph) should be greater, as should the need to lose such customers.

2.2.3 Recording the ABC sales: contribution chart

Use Figure 2.4 to record the sales and contributions of either all major markets/market segments or for principal customers. Some will be much more financially attractive and important than others.

FIGURE 2.4   The ABC sales: contribution proforma

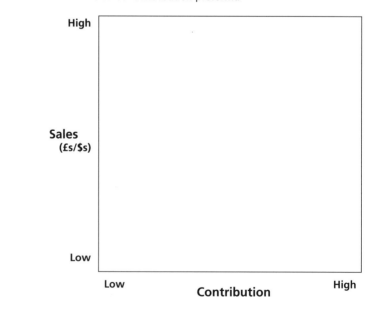

- **Locate each market, market segment, or principal customer on the sales: contribution chart.**

SUMMARY

These straightforward analyses have presented an important overview of the nature of existing customer groups or markets, their key characteristics, their relative importance in recent years to the organization, and their current value in terms of sales volume and contribution.

These analyses may demonstrate a need to re-think target market priorities and to keep abreast of a changing marketplace. If the examination of current markets has not prompted modifications to target market strategy and marketing programmes, the outcome from the analyses described in the remainder of Part Two probably will encourage changes.

There will be some significant strengths in the existing approach to customer targeting, and therefore to sales and marketing. These background analyses, plus some analyses detailed in the following pages, will highlight these strengths and help to ensure that this marketing planning exercise builds upon the organization's existing view of its marketplace and incorporates all that is currently relevant, up-to-date and best for the organization.

3

Market trends and the marketing environment

Having a sound understanding of trends in the marketplace is particularly important when re-assessing target markets and developing marketing plans. Markets or segments with current high volume and value should be targeted, together with those markets or segments likely to give the best future rewards. It is important not to continue supporting once-healthy markets that are now in a spiral of decline (see also Chapter 7). The general trends in the marketplace need to be considered, as do the drivers impacting on targeted customers, particularly in business-to-business marketing.

For all organizations, there are trading and market conditions over which the company has no direct control, but which do impact upon the company and its trading performance. These include issues relating to social pressures, legal, regulatory, political controls, technological changes, economic swings, plus more focused concerns of suppliers and competition, present opportunities and threats. These forces are termed *the marketing environment* and are examined in this chapter along with the statistical trends in different markets. This chapter will help the reader to:

- capture underlying market trends;
- appreciate the implications from the forces of the macro and micro marketing environment;
- identify opportunities and threats to address in the marketing plan.

3.1 MARKET TRENDS

A *market* is defined as an aggregate of people or businesses who have needs for products in a particular product class and who have the ability, willingness and authority to purchase such goods. Markets can be broken into segments: each *segment* consists of a sub-group of customers who share similar characteristics and buying behaviour, resulting in them having relatively similar product or service needs.

In order to plan and to make sound strategic decisions, there must also be an awareness of the numerical trends in the market:

- sales: volume size;
- sales: financial values;
- market size;
- market shares;
- numbers and sizes of customers;
- numbers of key competitors.

Figure 3.1 presents a summary chart for completion which captures this information.

FIGURE 3.1   Core market trends and predictions

Year	Sales volumes (units)	Sales £s/$s	Market size	Business's market share	Number of customers	Number of main competitors
2002						
2003						
2004						
2005						
2006						
2007						
2008						
2009						
2010						
2011						

- Complete as many columns as possible
- Information for 2008 (current year) onwards is based on predictions
- For many markets, the organization will not know market shares
- Principal customers: most businesses have an "80:20" split – the bulk of sales (e.g.: "80%") comes from a minority of customers (e.g.: "20%")
- Principal competitors (direct) indicate the level of market activity and to a degree, the "attractiveness" of the market

3.2 THE MARKETING ENVIRONMENT

The marketing environment is made up of those external forces that directly or indirectly influence an organisation's acquisitions of inputs and generation of outputs.

Dibb et al. 2006

In other words, these forces include aspects of the trading environment over which the organization has very little direct control, but which have the potential to tangibly affect the way in which the organization does business and performs.

Companies often have a good deal of relevant information at their disposal, but frequently this is poorly shared. This particular analysis, often referred to as a *PEST* analysis, makes sure the required information is pooled and incorporated within marketing strategy development.

To monitor changes in the marketing environment, marketers must scan and analyse continuously. Many companies have individual marketing managers or committees whose function is to collect and collate data related to trends in the market and aspects of the marketing environment. Sometimes a *PEST workshop* can be helpful, where a cross-functional team of managers, perhaps supplemented with external observers, brainstorms the important PEST variables and considers their implications. *Environmental scanning* is the process of tracking information from observation, secondary sources (particularly the trade press and government reports), databases, information services and marketing research, to examine each aspect of the PEST.

The marketing environment is generally broken into two key sections, termed the *macro* marketing environment and the *micro* marketing environment. All these aspects are external to the organization and outside its control. The broad macro forces impact upon all organizations operating in a particular market. The micro forces are largely competitive issues, which have a more variable or localized impact on individual organizations.

3.2.1 Macro marketing environment forces

The main elements are as follows.

Legal forces
Many laws influence marketing activities; for example: pro-competitive legislation and consumer protection legislation. The EU and NAFTA are big influences in this context.

Regulatory forces
Interpretation of laws is important, but so is an understanding of the enforcement by the various government ministries and local

government departments, plus the non-government regulatory bodies, such as GATT, or trade and professional associations.

Political forces

Many marketers view the actions of government as beyond influence, while others successfully lobby and influence the policy making and legislating bodies of central and local governments. It is important to remember that the lobbying of others can affect you.

Societal forces (culture)

These are the dynamics and workings of society: groups and individuals often ignore the activities of companies and marketers until they infringe their lifestyles and choices. An important current example is the Green movement and the notion of carbon footprints, which is leading consumers to pressurize companies to produce products that are less harmful to the earth's environment, create less waste and are produced in a more ecologically sensitive manner.

Technological forces

These refer to the technological expertise required to accomplish tasks and goals. Technology is quickly evolving and changing, affecting how people satisfy their needs and lead their lives. Technology is changing production, distribution, communications and selling, affecting the products marketers can bring to the marketplace and how they are presented to customers.

Economic conditions

General economic conditions – recession or boom – will impact upon any market, as will customer demand and spending behaviour. These are important considerations for any marketer, particularly as such conditions can be volatile, prone to dramatic changes, patterns and fashions.

3.2.2 Micro marketing environment forces

The elements of the micro marketing environment are aspects which are peculiar to an individual company/organization concerned, rather than market specific. However, they are also market factors over which the organization has little control. The key items to consider are as follows.

Direct and substitute competition

The nature and degree of competition in a particular product area from similar products are important aspects. Model proliferation is a competitive weapon used by major players such as Toshiba, IBM or HP. In addition, the possibility of competition from substitute products must be considered. Japanese-developed tunnelling robotic moles are a threat to traditional JCB or CAT diggers. A key question to consider is whether the market is stable or whether new kinds of competitors are emerging.

Supplier influence/power

Companies prefer independence and the opportunity to exert control over their suppliers. Yet control is not always possible: suppliers, particularly in situations where there are very few or if the products supplied are innovative or unique, can become uncomfortably strong. Cooperation may reduce the risks posed by such suppliers, but only if such relationships are stable.

The company's resource base

The resource base in terms of supplies and materials, finances, people, time and goodwill is generally in the control of the business itself. There are occasions, though, when trends in the marketplace and in the marketing environment act to strengthen or weaken the resource base. For example, new industry-wide working practices, legislation, altered banking policies, and customer pressures and demands, all alter the resource base. Activities which can affect the availability of resources must be closely monitored.

Customers' buying power

Customers' requirements and perceptions must constantly be monitored (see Chapter 5), but it is possible for underlying trends in the market to increase or decrease customer buying power. The result of either change will have a significant impact on the organization's performance and the likelihood of such changes in buying power must be checked.

No matter what the company or market, there are always elements of the marketing environment which directly impact on the competence of a company's performance and its ability to trade in a market.

3.3 MONITORING THE MARKETING ENVIRONMENT

At any one time in an organization not all of these aspects of the macro or micro marketing environment will be the centre of interest. But, some will, and perhaps others should! Often managers think about market trends and developments that may affect their organization, but they fail to articulate these concerns. In a marketing planning programme, such trends must be discussed. After all, the forces of the marketing environment will inevitably reveal opportunities to pursue, impact upon the choice of which markets to target, identify threats to address, dictate where products and brands should be positioned in the marketplace and how they should be placed in the marketing mix.

There are three approaches to undertaking an analysis of the marketing environment:

(a) Retain external consultants. While possible, this approach takes time and is costly. Experts with a detailed knowledge of the client organization, its markets, and the relevant marketing environment can be hard to find. Instead, it may be necessary to retain a number of consultants, with the associated obvious complications of cost, time, coordination and agreement of priorities.

(b) Allocate individual forces of the marketing environment to managers inside the organization or to small teams. These personnel should become the owners of 'their' part of the marketing environment, networking internally and externally with those having pertinent knowledge, expertise or insights. This approach works well, but only if (a) appropriate intranet and database systems are provided, and (b) regular forums are in place to enforce ownership, showcase the emerging issues and facilitate discussion.

(c) Stage an expert opinion workshop, harnessing the knowledge of a cross-functional set of managers and senior decision makers, supplemented with external industry observers and subject specialists. The 'brain-dumped' issues must be themed and then their implications – threat or opportunity – discussed. Finally, those themes deemed to be most important should be handed to separate work teams for further exploration and analysis, so that recommendations can subsequently be made. Such a workshop identified the following PEST issues for one of the world's leading car manufacturers. From this list six themes were identified for further examination.

Political/Regulatory/Legal	Economic	Social	Technological

● Eco-legislation
  – Emissions
  – Fuel use
  – Production processes
  – Waste
● Congestion charges and policy makers' reactions
● Open Door – China
● Trading blocs – protectionism
● World Trade Agreements and tariffs
	● Fuel prices
	● Lending rates
	● Debt equity ratios
	● Inflation
	● Role of China
	● Over-capacity
	● Manufacturer consolidation
	● Corporate down-sizing
	● Further expansion of Japanese players – Lexus in Europe
		● Lifestyle needs – growing role impacting on car KCVs
		● Lifestyle demands on home/garden/ travel spending
		● Role of media in altering the public's aspirations
		● Security concerns
		● Demographic changes
		● Growing number of adult singles
			● Consumer desire for innovation
			● Product quality drivers
			● Productivity drivers
			● Internet access to information
			● Customer management systems
			● Hybrid drive systems
			● Lighter chassis and skin materials
			● Recycling requirements

Political/Regulatory/Legal	**Economic**	**Social**	**Technological**
<ul><li>Alliances encouraged to exploit developing economies</li><li>Working hours' directives</li><li>Terrorism atrocities</li></ul>	<ul><li>Diesel's growth in Europe</li><li>Further strategic alliances</li><li>Company car taxation/role</li></ul>	<ul><li>Changing role of female purchasing</li><li>Decline of US luxury market</li><li>Environmental impact publicity</li><li>Eco-diffusion</li></ul>	<ul><li>Supply chain sharing with rivals</li><li>Supply chain consolidation</li></ul>

Marketing environment trends likely to affect the organization need to be summarized (see Figure 3.2). This chart is a simple statement of issues thought likely to be important. Once complete, the leading issues can be prioritized and examined further. Individual managers will need to be allocated to look into separate issues and trends. A particular

FIGURE 3.2   The marketing environment issues

Summary of core issues

Macro environment
(legal, regulatory and political, societal, technological, economic)

Micro environment
(direct and substitute competition, new entrants, supplier influence, customer
  buying power)

Principal implications to the organization of these issues

- Consider the wide range of potentially relevant aspects
- Be prudent and objective – list only important concerns
- List the most pressing/crucial issues first
- Have evidence to support these assertions
- Have facts with sources with which to defend statements

priority is to identify emerging threats and opportunities. Awareness of marketing environment developments may provide first mover advantages vis-à-vis rivals and minimize threats. To ignore these market developments and trends is very foolish. The main issues identified should feed into the organization's SWOT analysis, featured next in *Marketing Planning*.

The authors' textbook website for their title *Marketing: Concepts and Strategies* provides further explanation for conducting an analysis of the marketing environment. Access this at www.dibbmarketing.com, select the 'Student Section' in the menu, then *Practitioners' Use of Key Analytical Tools*. From the sub-menu, select 'Analysing the Marketing Environment'.

SUMMARY

The analyses presented in this chapter have examined the statistical trends in the core markets as well as the general marketing environment issues likely to have an impact upon the organization, its suppliers, competitors and customers. While the organization may have little direct influence over these factors, they nevertheless must be tackled if the business is to perform as desired.

The statistical trends are an important reflection of the organization's performance, its stature in its markets and its likely potential: sales volume/value, market size/share, number and size of leading customers and the coverage of distribution. The wider marketing environment includes legal, regulatory, political, societal, technological and economic macro forces, plus the more micro concerns of direct competition, substitutes, supplier influence and customer buying power. To avoid damaging surprises and to maximize opportunities, these issues must be monitored and evaluated.

4

SWOT analysis: strengths, weaknesses, opportunities and threats

One of the simplest and most widely deployed of the marketing analyses, the SWOT analysis, can sometimes prove to be misleading, overly subjective and of little strategic value. However, by applying certain rules, this examination of the organization's capabilities, opportunities and threats plays a crucial role in the creation of a robust marketing plan. Marketing planning seeks to identify opportunities to pursue while leveraging the organization's capabilities to best effect. Without an honest assessment of strengths and weaknesses, decisions about which opportunities and which target markets to prioritize may be misguided and over-optimistic. Marketing plans should also propose remedies for weaknesses and seek to pre-empt threats. The SWOT analysis is an integral part of producing an effective marketing plan. This chapter aims to:

- ensure the organization's capabilities guide recommendations in the marketing plan;
- identify weaknesses to remedy in the marketing plan's actions;
- determine opportunities and threats to address in the plan's recommendations and programmes.

4.1 THE SWOT ANALYSIS

The SWOT (or the alternative matrix, TOWS) analysis is one of the most commonly implemented analyses in marketing. It is also widely used in other disciplines such as total quality management (TQM). A simple format for presentation is illustrated in Figure 4.1: Strengths, Weaknesses, Opportunities and Threats. Strengths and weaknesses are issues *internal* to an organization, while opportunities and threats relate to *external* aspects of the marketplace (many of which stem from an analysis of the marketing environment, as described in the previous

FIGURE 4.1 The SWOT grid

	Strengths	Weaknesses
Internal		
External	Opportunities	Threats

chapter). It is important that the SWOT analysis is not merely a collection of managers' hunches. It must be based on objective facts and on marketing research findings. The SWOT analysis should (a) focus on the most crucial 'hot' issues, and (b) be relative to the strongest competitors in a particular market. The SWOT gives a clear picture of the organization's situation and where action is required to maximize opportunities and minimize threats and weaknesses.

Managers often produce an overall summary SWOT, but may also prepare separate ones for major business units, product groups, brands and key target markets. Marketing-oriented organizations sometimes also produce SWOT grids for each leading competitor and for separate markets. This helps to reveal a company's relative strengths and weaknesses and pinpoints its ability to face the identified threats and opportunities. Role-playing a key competitor and producing its SWOT can be a highly revealing exercise, identifying the nature of the challenge posed by the competitor but also revealing how best to expose its weaknesses.

4.2 ISSUES: INTERNAL ENVIRONMENT – STRENGTHS/ WEAKNESSES

A SWOT analysis can include a range of different issues, but typically for internal issues, such as Strengths and Weaknesses, will centre on the following areas.

Marketing

Product	Service/people
Pricing	Distribution/distributors
Promotion	Branding and positioning
Marketing information/intelligence	Resources

Engineering and product development

Often this area is of peripheral importance but as the level of formalized input from the marketing function increases (such as in many manufacturing organizations), this is changing.

Operations

Production/engineering	Processing orders/transactions
Sales and marketing	Economies of scale

People

R&D	Sales
Distributors	After sales/service
Marketing	Processing/customer service

People's skills, wages/benefits, training and development, motivation, conditions, and turnover are all aspects central to the successful implementation of the customer-focused marketing philosophy and the marketing strategy.

Management

Sometimes a sensitive and contentious area, it is nonetheless the case that management structures, behaviours and philosophies occasionally need altering to facilitate the successful implementation of a marketing strategy. Such issues and problems should be raised within the SWOT, so that remedies emerge in the marketing plan's recommendations. Possibly also strategic alliances, partnerships, mergers and other structural issues should be cited.

Company resources

The following resources are particularly worthy of note:

- people and skills;
- finance (budgets);
- scheduling.

4.3 ISSUES: EXTERNAL ENVIRONMENT – THREATS/ OPPORTUNITIES

These issues relate strongly to the marketing environment (see Chapter 3). The core features to consider include:

- Social/cultural;
- Regulatory/legal/political;
- Technological;
- Economic conditions;
- Competition:
  - global players,
  - international versus national versus local,
  - intensity of rivalry,
  - ability,
  - threat of entry,
  - pressure from substitutions,
  - market's customer needs,
  - bargaining power of buyers, distributors, suppliers.

From a thorough SWOT analysis, an organization can glean initial insights into distinctive competencies and differential advantages over rivals; customer needs; product portfolio requirements; competitive positioning; assumptions on which strategic decisions will be based; the match of the company's status with stated corporate goals; as well as the more obvious remarks concerning marketing opportunities and threats, company strengths and weaknesses.

4.4 CONDUCTING THE SWOT

For each target market or market segment under review, list the most important (of most concern/likely influence on the performance of the organization) issues in each of the four elements of the SWOT grid – Strengths, Weaknesses, Opportunities and Threats. See Figure 4.2.

In each of the four SWOT sections, ensure that the points are listed in ranked order of importance: for example, put the number one threat first, and so on. This approach adds considerable clarity to the resulting SWOT. Be specific, rather than rely on a simple word: for example 'performance' is often cited as a strength, but the underlying details making performance a strength should be the points stated in the SWOT. There is no point listing dozens of issues: emphasize only those points of most impact upon the company. Note that the points listed should take account of the organization's position versus its strongest rivals. Be objective: the assertions should be backed up with evidence (quotations, letters, trade statistics, press reports, government publications, sales force feedback, customer comments) or not included. The key implications from the analysis of the marketing environment should feature in the SWOT's opportunities and threats.

Try to seek the views of a cross-section of colleagues and external pundits or analysts. Finally, rather than the analysis being little more

F I G U R E 4 . 2 The SWOT analysis

Strengths	Weaknesses

Opportunities	Threats

- Rank (list) points in order of importance
- Only include key points/issues
- Have evidence to support these points or exclude them
- Strengths and Weaknesses should be relative to main competitors
- Strengths and Weaknesses are *internal* issues
- Opportunities and Threats are *external* marketing environment issues

What are the core implications from these issues?

than an interesting 'brain dump' of thoughts and issues, ensure that the implications from these key SWOT points are explored, so that appropriate actions are recommended in the marketing plan. The result should be clarity about which strengths to emphasize in sales and marketing programmes, which opportunities are the most important pursuits, how to remedy the weaknesses competitors might effectively exploit, and which threats must be pre-empted or combated in subsequent marketing programmes.

The authors' textbook website for their title *Marketing: Concepts and Strategies* provides further explanation for conducting a SWOT analysis. Access this at www.dibbmarketing.com, select the 'Student Section' in the menu, then *Practitioners' Use of Key Analytical Tools*. From the sub-menu, select 'Undertaking a SWOT Analysis'.

SUMMARY

This chapter has reviewed the development of the SWOT analysis. This simple approach allows companies to review the opportunities present in the marketplace and weigh up their capabilities for pursuing them. An appreciation of the threats that are likely to impact upon the organization's position can also be achieved. Adopting a customer-focused view of strengths and weaknesses helps to ensure realistic decisions are made about where to direct resources, helping the organization to make the best of available opportunities. It is essential that marketing plan recommendations rectify key weaknesses and deficiencies.

To avoid the SWOT analysis becoming misleadingly subjective and simplistic, it is necessary to adhere to certain 'house rules'. Lists should be prioritized, only points for which there is some credible evidence may be included, strengths and weaknesses must be benchmarked against strong competitors, opportunities and threats should be informed by the analysis of the marketing environment, the views of a broad set of stakeholders are required. The implications of the included issues must be debated, so that informed recommendations emerge in the marketing plan.

5

Customer needs, expectations and buying processes

Organizations can only know which customers to target and understand which marketing programmes will appeal to these customers, by developing a clear understanding of the needs and buying behaviour of their customer base. This involves understanding the number, types and characteristics of customers in a particular market, reviewing the buying process, understanding who is involved in this decision making, identifying influences on the buying process, monitoring emerging trends and identifying current perceptions of different brands and patterns of supplier loyalty. A robust understanding of these areas is vital to effective marketing and an essential component of a strong marketing plan. This chapter seeks to:

- develop a complete understanding of customers, their needs and buying behaviour;
- provide the required insights into business customers or consumers to determine a targeting strategy;
- establish ways in which the marketing plan must strive to satisfy targeted customers.

5.1 INSIGHTS INTO CUSTOMERS

Many companies find that they must cater for the needs of a variety of different customer types. Any organization operating in a wide range of markets must deal with customer diversity on a daily basis. Satisfying so varied a customer base involves having a sound understanding of what product, service, sales and marketing attributes customers expect and need. Companies vary in their ability to track customer histories and data. Even those which regularly update such records often fail to fully understand why customers make a particular purchase or enter into a relationship with a certain supplier in preference to another.

Developing marketing programmes which strongly appeal to target customers, requires that companies fully appreciate the needs of their customer base. This means understanding the number, types and characteristics of customers in a particular market, reviewing the buying process and influences on each customer type, keeping a close eye on emerging trends and identifying current perceptions of different brands and patterns of supplier loyalty. Business customers or consumers, whichever is a particular organization's focus, rarely 'stand still' in terms of their expectations and perceptions of what is being offered. Updating insights into customers' needs, behaviours and perceptions is therefore essential. The annual marketing planning season is a perfect opportunity to either update such customer knowledge or ensure marketing programmes fully reflect customers' issues.

Keeping historical records of customer numbers and types was discussed in Chapters 2 and 3, while Section 8.5 will deal with reviewing customer perceptions of competing products and brands. The aims of this chapter are to review customer characteristics, consider the buying process which customers go through when they buy, look at the factors which impact upon the buying decision and examine the product/ service requirements (Key Customer Values or KCVs) of different customer types.

5.2 UNDERSTANDING CUSTOMERS AND KEY CUSTOMER VALUES

A clear understanding of customer needs and requirements is central to any marketing strategy or marketing planning programme. The marketing concept, after all, hinges on ensuring the customer is the focus of decision making. If companies are to capitalize on customer needs and take advantage of marketing opportunities, a detailed profile of those requirements is vital. For example, it is essential to understand the precise mix of product characteristics, service support, pricing and payment terms, channel delivery and promotion required by each customer type. Any uncertainty may result in less effective marketing programmes being developed.

When reviewing the needs of different customer types it is helpful to ask the following questions:

- What benefits is the customer seeking from the product or service? Are these benefits tangible or intangible?

- Does the customer have any other needs which are related to the product or service in question? How do these affect the purchasing decision?

- Is the purchase of any other product or service linked to that being reviewed?
- What criteria does the customer consider when making the purchase decision? For example, how important are issues such as quality, delivery, service, price, product range, product innovation, brand reputation and the influence of promotional activity in the decision?
- What supplier criteria does the customer use when choosing what to buy?
- How does the customer go about searching for product or service information? For example, which media, publications, trade shows and exhibitions, word-of-mouth recommendations, etc. are used?
- What role does brand identity and awareness play?
- What is the impact of the customer's previous experiences?
- How does the customer identify and select the competitive set or options available?
- Who else is involved in the decision making or as an influencing agent?

5.2.1 Key Customer Values (KCVs)

Some of these questions relate specifically to customer needs or Key Customer Values (KCVs), as they are sometimes known. KCVs are those factors expected and considered most important by customers. If these are not offered, the customer may not make a purchase, or may buy an alternative product which comes closer to matching their needs. The answers to the other questions are helpful when marketing programmes are designed for different customer segments.

An understanding of KCVs is essential if an organization is to genuinely satisfy its targeted customers and endeavour to fend off its competitors. The 'voice of the customer' must be heard when determining product portfolios and new product development. Current NPD management practices such as quality functional deployment (QFD) depend on this knowledge of customer needs and expectations. Identifying KCVs is the base entry point for a marketer seeking to understand customers. Marketers, brand managers, customer service staff, the sales force and business development managers will all be able to provide valuable insights into these KCVs, but the views of customers are also required!

5.2.2 Customer profiles

The design of effective marketing programmes is contingent upon having a clear profile of the characteristics of different customer types. Many companies find that it is helpful to formally sketch a brief profile of key customer types at the same time as developing a list of key customer values. Indeed, the notion that certain customer characteristics are linked with specific needs and requirements is a central concept in effective target marketing and marketing planning.

5.2.3 Buying process and influences

As well as having a sound appreciation of KCVs, selling organizations must properly understand how and why individual customers and organizations buy. This is because the mechanics of buying tend to impact on the nature of the KCVs required. Understanding the buying process and the mechanics (steps) involved helps companies to tailor their marketing efforts to more effectively influence the buying decision. In short, this allows a more suitable marketing mix (product, price, distribution, promotion and people) to be developed for the customers targeted.

5.3 THE BEHAVIOUR AND BUYING PROCESSES OF CUSTOMERS

When discussing the behaviour and buying mechanics of customers, it is necessary to distinguish between individual and organizational buyers. Thus consumer buyer behaviour is said to comprise the decision processes and acts of individuals involved in buying and using products or services; that is, you and me. Organizational (business-to-business) buyer behaviour is said to represent the purchase behaviour of other producers and re-sellers, government units and institutions; that is, where the customer is not an end-user consumer. The customer portfolios of companies always vary in terms of the types of customers they include.

5.3.1 Consumer buying decision process

There have been many attempts to model or map out the way that individuals buy. Figure 5.1 illustrates a format which is typical of those which have been developed.

Briefly, the consumer buying decision process holds that consumers first recognize a problem or need for a product or service; they then search for information about relevant options (based on previous experiences, memory, KCVs, media and marketing influences); options are then evaluated against the KCVs/benchmarks set by each consumer; and the purchase is made (quickly for a routine purchase and with more care for a risky, expensive or infrequently replaced item). The process does not end there, though, as consumers constantly assess the performance and suitability of their purchase: such views will influence the eventual replacement/renewal purchase.

FIGURE 5.1   Consumer buying decision process and possible influences

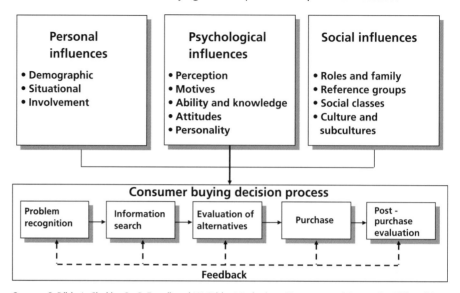

Source: S. Dibb, L. Simkin, O. C. Ferrell and W. Pride, *Marketing: Concepts and Strategies,* Fifth edition. Copyright © 2006 Houghton Mifflin Company. Used with permission.

There are a number of factors which *influence* the way in which people buy. By understanding the range of these factors, organizations are in a better position to develop marketing programmes which cater for the consumers. These influencing factors can be grouped in the following way:

- *Person specific influences*. Demographic issues (age/sex/occupation/ income) and situational factors (external conditions which exist when a purchase is made).

- *Psychological influences*. Consumers' different perceptions, motives and attitudes towards what and how they purchase, illustrated by the Green movement's purchasing behaviour.

- *Social influences*. Purchases made by consumers are influenced by a range of social factors. For example, individual tastes are influenced by social class and culture. Similarly, how consumers behave is affected by family roles and reference groups (friends/colleagues).

- *Media influences*. Explicit marketing-led media activity such as advertising, sales promotion, publicity, sponsorship and direct mail obviously must influence purchase behaviour, but so do broadcast and print news, current affairs, drama and even light entertainment messages.

The benefits of understanding how and why customers buy have already been explored. By mapping out the process in this way, it is possible to refine the marketing efforts which are made at each stage of the buying decision.

5.3.2 The organizational or business-to-business decision process

Organizational markets can be classified into:

- *Industrial or producer markets*: these companies buy products for use in the manufacture of other products or to support that manufacture. For example, Nestlé buys glucose syrup/cocoa powder/ sugar, etc.

- *Re-seller markets*: companies in this category buy goods for re-sale to customers. Generally they do not alter the physical nature of those goods, but they add value in terms of location/availability, warranty, service, parts support, relationships with customers. For example, wholesalers or retailers, such as Marks and Spencer or Aldi. A sub-category includes those organizations which do not buy from a supplier, taking ownership, but which do sell on behalf of suppliers: agents, distributors or dealers, such as car franchisees or JCB depots. These companies deal in physical goods.

- *Institutional markets*: companies in this category include charities, libraries, hospitals, colleges.

- *Government markets*: this category includes both local and national government and their agencies. These companies are generally involved with the handling of services.

This distinction into organizational type is important because it affects the characteristics of the buying process. For instance, government markets are known for their bureaucratic buying processes, often operating through a series of committees seeking tenders, taking many months. Various attempts have been made to model the organizational buying decision process. Figure 5.2 is typical of the formats which have been developed.

The business-to-business buying decision process is similar to that for individual consumers, but typically is more formal. Once a need is recognized for a product or service, a specification is drawn up prior to a screening of potential suppliers. Those short-listed suppliers are ranked and assessed in terms of costs, reliability/reputation, product know-how, logistical support, service levels, etc. There is also an element of post-purchase evaluation, even when regular contracts are instigated.

There is a range of factors which impact on and *influence* the nature of buying and how that buying takes place. These include:

- *Environmental*: such as laws, regulations, economic conditions, social issues, competitive forces and technological change. For example, the impact of EU deregulation and more freedom to buy.

- *Organizational*: including company objectives (which may be short or long term), purchasing policies (such as 'Buy British'), resources, and the structure of the buying centre.

FIGURE 5.2   Model of the organizational or business-to-business buying process

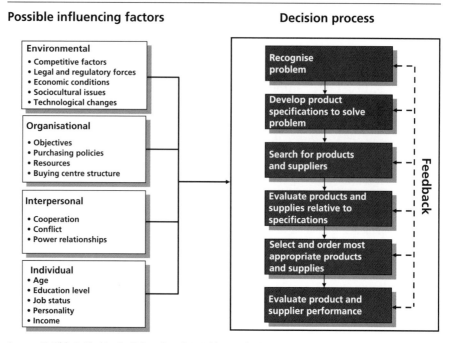

Source: S. Dibb, L. Simkin, O. C. Ferrell and W. Pride, *Marketing: Concepts and Strategies*, Fifth edition. Copyright © 2006 Houghton Mifflin Company. Used with permission.

- *Interpersonal*: anyone involved in buying for an organization will understand the power of relationships, conflict and cooperation which can impact on the decisions made.
- *Individual*: as in consumer buying, individual factors such as age, education level and job status or risk will have an impact on the choices which are made.

5.3.3 Organizational versus consumer buyer behaviour

There are a number of obvious contrasts between consumer buying behaviour and the behaviour exhibited by organizations. These can be shown by highlighting the particular characteristics of organizational or business-to-business buyer behaviour and influences.

Group activity

Generally more people are involved in organizational buying behaviour than in consumer buying behaviour. Those involved in buying in a business-to-business situation are collectively referred to as the *Buying Centre* and each individual will be responsible for particular buying roles. The number of people involved in buying will be organization-specific, but usually relates to the type of purchase being made, the risk associated with it and budget/time pressures.

High risk

Buying for organizations is usually more high risk than consumer purchase. Risk in organizational purchases can come from high product value, the possible consequence of purchase, lack of knowledge about the product or service being bought, and uncertainty about the buying process or how to deal with suppliers.

Fewer and larger buyers

Fast Moving Consumer Goods (FMCG) companies tend to aim their products at more 'mass' markets or segments consisting of tens of thousands of consumers, but many companies in business-to-business markets are reliant on relatively few customers. This means there is a tendency for long-term relationships to be developed, with organizations seeking the benefits of reduced risk, trust, mutual adaptation, time saving, etc. and there is more use of personal selling (face-to-face contact).

Formal buying process

Organizational buyers are often restricted by certain company rules or procedures and have a fairly limited say in the purchase which is made. Some organizations are particularly bureaucratic. Generally, there is extensive use of formal quotes and tenders, and long-term contracts.

Nature of demand

Demand in organizational markets is derived from demand for products or services in consumer markets. This means it tends to fluctuate according to the level of demand for consumer goods (for example the demand for glucose syrup is affected by the demand for confectionery).

Geographic concentration of buyers

There is a tendency for a concentration of certain industries to occur in one area. For example, in the UK, IT suppliers are now centred along the M4 motorway corridor, defence companies concentrate around Bristol, automotive component companies tend to locate around major car producing plants.

5.4 ASSESSING CUSTOMERS, KCVs, BUYING PROCESSES IN THE BUYING PROFORMA

At this stage in the marketing planning process and associated analyses, it is necessary to add to the historical and quantitative picture of customers developed in Chapters 2 and 3. For each type or group of customers a more qualitative profile is needed. As part of the authors' approach to developing market segments, the *Dibb/Simkin Buying Proforma* was created for their *Market Segmentation Workbook* in the early 1990s. This built on the accepted best practice principles from the buying behaviour literature and, over the years, has proved very successful in portraying the nature of the customer challenge. By completing this proforma, marketers reveal most of what is needed about their customers. These issues must be addressed in a marketing plan.

Typically the *Buying Proforma* is completed by a mix of marketing, sales and customer service managers. It is essential that the views of managers who regularly interact with customers are included. The completed proformas – one for each target market or market segment – should be verified by gaining the views of a sample of customers. It can be very cost-effective and time-efficient to hand the proformas to a qualitative marketing research organization for validation in a few focus groups or interviews.

Using a copy of the Dibb/Simkin Buying Proforma in Figure 5.3 for *each customer group or target market*, make a record of:

FIGURE 5.3 Customers, KCVs, buying process steps and core influences – the buying proforma

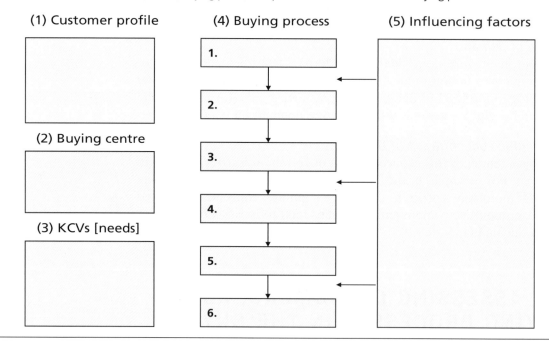

- Record the buying process, influences on each stage, typical customer profile and KCVs for each customer group or market segment. Start in the left-hand column and work across left-to-right
- Number the *Influences* and indicate on the arrows which *Influences* apply to each separate step in the *Buying Process*
- Note: the KCVs should match Figure 2.1 and be listed in order of importance to the customer
- A worked example appears on p. 43

© Sally Dibb & Lyndon Simkin

(i) *Customer profile.* Build up a picture of the typical characteristics of the customer type under review. Include any relevant personality, demographic, location, situational details.

(ii) *Buying centre composition.* Identify who is involved in the purchase and their respective roles.

(iii) *Key customer values.* Make a list of the KCVs required by each customer group (see Figure 2.1). These should be listed in order of importance to the customer.

(iv) *The buying process mechanics.* List out the steps involved in the buying process (from the customer's viewpoint). What steps does the customer go through in order to make the purchase?

(v) *The core influences.* Record any factors which have an influence on the buying decision being made. Which factors/issues influence *each* step in the process described (see iv)?

FIGURE 5.4   Example of a completed buying proforma

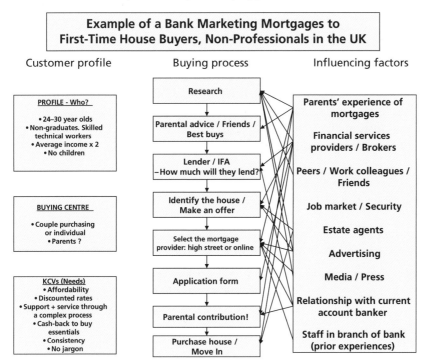

© Sally Dibb & Lyndon Simkin

The authors' textbook website for their title *Marketing: Concepts and Strategies* provides further explanation for conducting an analysis of customers and using the Dibb/Simkin Buying Proforma. Access this at www.dibbmarketing.com, select the 'Student Section' in the menu, then *Practitioners' Use of Key Analytical Tools*. From the sub-menu, select 'Using the Dibb/Simkin Buying Proforma to Understand Customers' Buying Behaviour'.

SUMMARY

This chapter has developed an understanding of business customers' or consumers' buying behaviour: essential for any successful marketing activity but critical for the production of a meaningful marketing plan. This important area of marketing analysis is often overlooked, yet it provides a valuable insight into customer needs which goes further than simply considering product requirements. By examining the mechanics of buying it is possible to develop an entire marketing offering which is geared to satisfying customer requirements from the point at which unfulfilled need is recognized right up to the point of consumption. An appreciation of the core influences on buying should assist the business in determining which of these influences it is important to try to control or direct. This additional understanding can be particularly important in markets where there is little variety in product needs or where competition is especially intense. In these circumstances, using buying behaviour characteristics to distinguish between different customer groups may offer an opportunity for developing a differential advantage over rivals.

Without a thorough appreciation of customers' needs, buying behaviour and perceptions, it is not possible to adequately practise marketing or develop effective marketing plans. Arguably, without such insights, it is not feasible to expect to fend off competitors or for the organization to survive!

6

Competition and competitors' strategies

Marketing planning decisions must fully consider the prevailing competitive situation in which the company operates. The success of marketing programmes are contingent upon an organization competing effectively. This means that an excellent understanding of the strategies, capabilities and programmes of rivals is required. There seems little doubt that marketing success is closely linked with becoming 'competitor orientated'. Not surprisingly, successful marketing planning also relies on having a sound understanding of competitors' relative strengths and weaknesses, market shares, positionings and their intentions. By combining knowledge about the competitive situation with an understanding of key customer needs, organizations are better able to pinpoint attractive segments and position their product offerings. Closely monitoring change in the competitive arena helps organizations to maintain control over their target market strategy and marketing plans. Failure to understand the threat posed by competitors can lead to commercial ruin. This chapter will help the reader to:

- understand the nature of the competitive threat;
- assess how to attack or defend;
- apply the principles of warfare strategy in the marketing context.

6.1 UNDERSTANDING THE COMPETITIVE ARENA

American management guru Michael Porter considers the competitive arena to consist of competing organizations jockeying for position in an environment determined by a number of outside forces (see Figure 6.1). Porter argues that too many organizations only assess their like-for-like

FIGURE 6.1 Industry forces in the competitive arena

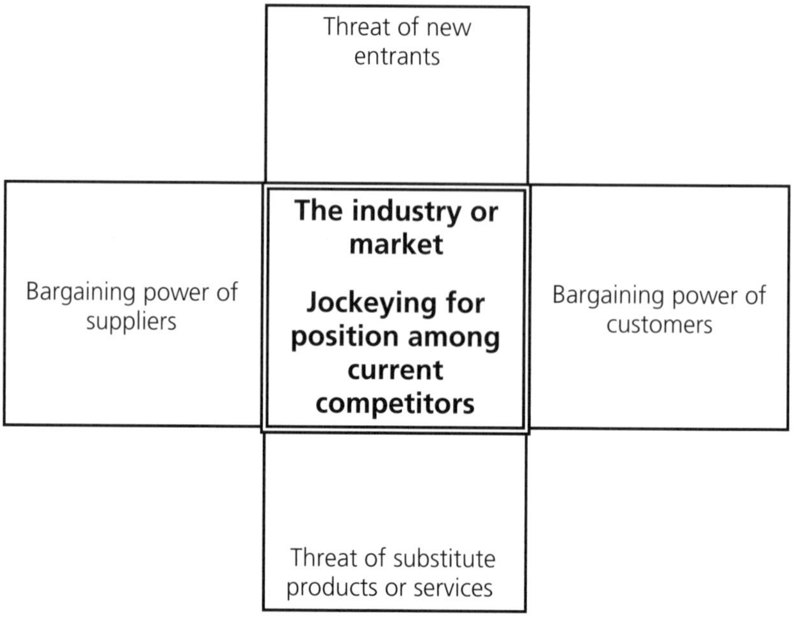

Source: Michael Porter (1979), *How Competitive Forces Shape Strategy,* Harvard Business Review 47, 137–145.
See also: *Competitive Strategy* and *Competitive Advantage,* both by Michael Porter (2004) The Free Press: New York.

rivals, ignoring other competitive forces such as emerging new entrants or substitute solutions to customers' requirements. Understanding the competitive context should go much deeper than descriptive assessments of a rival's products, pricing and promotional messages.

Bargaining power of suppliers
How much a particular supplier impacts upon a company's competitive situation depends on the availability of alternative suppliers and product substitutes. In monopoly situations the bargaining power of the supplier is particularly strong and may be associated with high prices and inflexible, poor quality, product offerings. At the other extreme, supplying companies in industries with many suppliers and much substitution frequently have quite low bargaining power. In general, the relative power of one supplier vis-à-vis its competitors will vary with consequent impact upon the basis for competing.

Bargaining power of buyers
High buyer bargaining power usually occurs in industries where suppliers' power is low and where large volumes of standardized items can readily be sourced elsewhere. In many cases these items form only a part of the final product. The bargaining power of buyers may vary across competing suppliers.

Threat of substitute products or services

Direct rivals are not the only threat: customers may turn to a substitute or alternative type of solution and provider. A proliferation of substitute products within an industry can significantly limit the growth potential and long-term profits. This results in competing companies having less control over price and possibly facing over-capacity problems. It is worth noting that when a company thinks it has first mover advantage and that it has developed something to offer customers ahead of any rivals, invariably it is acting as a substitute competitor for how ever the customer's problem or need is currently met.

Threat of new entrants

New entrants in a market give increased capacity which can limit the market share or profits of existing competitors. The likely impact of new entrants is partly determined by barriers to entry. Some typical barriers to entry include the presence of strongly branded competitors, economies of scale, control of distribution and high capital requirements. In markets where barriers are high, the number of new entrants will be limited. It is usually known in an industry when a new competitor is intending to launch, so there should be the opportunity to look at the impending new entrant's other markets in order to deduce probable strategy and marketing programmes.

It is often valuable to ask customers about the competing products or brands they considered and why. Often there are some surprises in the responses provided: perhaps including substitute solutions or technologies. It is important to take time to identify the competitive set. Having done so, the capabilities and performance of competitors should be assessed to judge their probable threat. All too often organizations do little more than subjectively describe rivals' marketing mixes. This is not sufficient: instead there needs to be an appreciation of competitors' strategies and intentions, decision-making, target marketing, resourcing and programmes, as well as their basis for competing and whether they possess the *Holy Grail* of marketing, a competitive advantage.

Porter believes there are three bases on which to compete, in order to achieve a competitive advantage. An organization which *fails* to master any one of these is *un*likely to have the strengths with which to fend off competitors. Unfortunately, many organizations master none of these bases, instead operating without any real edge, and becoming vulnerable to lower cost rivals, better differentiated competitors, or organizations which are more focused. Porter's three 'generic routes' for achieving competitive advantage are as follows.

i) Cost leadership

This involves a low cost base achieved through scale economies of production and experience – Toyota's or Aldi's approach. Only the organization with the lowest cost base and most extensive learning economies can sustain this option. Any other company seeking to differentiate itself with lowest price products or services risks being under-cut by the lowest cost competitor. This makes low price a risky approach to seeking an edge over rivals.

ii) Differentiation

Here a unique product or marketing offer is at the heart of the competitive strategy. This can be achieved through the development of an innovative product, service, branding, distribution or pricing – Caterpillar aims to be a 'one stop shop' in construction equipment through having the most extensive product range and distribution coverage; BMW differentiates on the basis of driving experience; while easyJet differentiates through low prices.

iii) Focus

This approach is often adopted by smaller companies unable to opt for *Cost* or *Differentiation*, and which specialize in tightly defined markets or product groups. It is possible to build up a reputation as a specialist in targeted markets, but such nichers are vulnerable if these customers defect elsewhere or if mainstream competitors decide to serve the same niche. Porsche has a focused strategy.

6.2 WARFARE STRATEGIES

The analysis of competition and the development of competitive strategies have been linked to military principles. Under this scenario, competing companies represent the *enemy* which must be defeated. In any market or market segment, there are said to be five different types of competitive positions that companies may occupy. Which position a company occupies, and how this fits in with what the competition is doing, will impact upon the strategy which that company should follow.

6.2.1 Competitive positions

There are five possible positions for an organization. Placing rivals into these positions and populating the competitive positions proforma are at the heart of conducting a meaningful competitor analysis and to ascertaining on what basis to establish competitive advantage.

Market leader

This is the highest market share company which retains its position by (i) trying to expand the total market, perhaps by finding new uses for a product, or (ii) increasing market share (market penetration), for example through an aggressive advertising campaign, and (iii) defending current markets and satisfied customers. Market leading companies need to achieve a balance between aggressively seeking new market share while protecting their existing position.

Market challengers

This position is occupied by one or more non-market leaders which want to occupy the position of market leader with the largest market share. A challenger *aggressively* attacks for additional market share, devoting resources to marketing programmes targeted at competitors. Branson and Virgin challenged BA in the airline wars between the UK and the USA, devoting significant resources to Virgin Atlantic's customer service and marketing programmes.

Market followers

These are low share competitors without the resources/market position/R&D/commitment to challenge or seriously contend for market leadership. Instead they are happy to settle for a smaller share of the market. They plod along, but in highly aggressive markets they are very vulnerable to more innovative and powerful competitors.

Fast movers

Fast movers are very low share rivals, but they are growing relatively quickly. Currently they are minor players, but smart strategies and targeted spending may well create significant growth in business levels. Fast movers should be attacked before they have grown their market share and are safe.

Market nichers

These are companies which specialize in terms of market/product/customers by finding a safe, profitable market segment. As markets mature, increasing competitiveness forces larger rivals to target such segments, making life difficult for the nicher. Companies which commit all their resources to one niche market can find themselves particularly susceptible in such circumstances.

Why are competitive positions important? Quite simply, different marketing strategies are appropriate depending upon the competitive position. Nichers specialize and are narrowly focused. Market leaders have to fend off competitors' attacks while continuing plans to develop and grow their markets. Challengers are aggressive but must only attack the leader's and other challengers' weak points: head-on moves will most likely be costly. Followers are the 'me-toos' in the marketplace: they copy other players' successes. Fast movers are often innovative and very flexible. The various marketing strategies may be based either on attacking or defensive moves.

6.2.2 Principles of defensive warfare strategies

The skill to adopt a defensive position is important if companies are to protect their existing market share. However, defence should not be regarded solely as a negative activity. Strong defence involves striking a balance between waiting to be attacked and responding to aggressive competitive moves. In general, only the market leader should consider adopting a highly defensive role, but even for this player, it is essential to combine defensive and offensive strategies. Nichers, once established, may become defensive in nature. Some companies fall into a false sense of security about their market position and leave themselves open to attack from aggressive market challengers. Such companies should remember that adopting a defensive position does not necessarily mean remaining static; they should be ready to move and respond to aggressive marketing effort from competitors. Defence still presents several options:

- *Build walls around strong positions*. This requires companies to fully understand their true strengths (for example, brand name), and to be proactive in their attempts to retain those strengths.

- *Protect weak areas*. Attention on weak areas can sometimes be diverted by marketing tactics which focus on other aspects of the product/marketing offering.

- *Be mobile and ready to move*. Companies should be quick to exploit new markets, products and opportunities.

- *Withdraw from a market/product if absolutely necessary*. It can be sensible to consolidate in areas which are strong, thus focusing resources. Such action should not leave weak areas which might allow competitors access to other key markets.

6.2.3 Principles of offensive warfare strategies

The principles of offensive warfare are particularly relevant to companies in a non-market leading position, which are challenging aggressively for additional market share, such as challengers and fast movers. Attacking market followers and market nichers is often seen as lower risk than tackling the market leading organization, but this depends on the strength of the leader's position. Challenging companies must beware the dangers of antagonizing powerful, resource-rich market leaders and other strong challengers. If the leader is to be attacked, the challenging organization must find a weakness in the leader's strength and attack at that point. Launching the attack on a narrow front tends to increase the chances of success. The challenger should be sure that it has the resources to sustain the attack for as long as necessary.

- *Head to head*. This full frontal method of attack is in many ways the most difficult to sustain and only the most powerful challengers should attempt it. The attack involves attempting to match the market leader blow by blow on some aspect of the marketing programme (for example, price). Challengers that attempt this approach often fail!

- *Attack weak points*. This approach requires the challenger to identify and match its key areas of strength and weakness against the market leader. Efforts can then be pitched against points of particular weakness.

- *Adopt a multi-pronged strategy.* It may be appropriate to overwhelm competitors with several points of attack (for example, combining a promotional programme with new product innovation), and thus diluting competitors' ability to respond.
- *Guerrilla attack.* This type of challenging is not large scale nor prolonged. The intention is to annoy competitors with unpredictable and periodic attacks.

6.2.4 Strategies for market followers, nichers and fast movers

There are opportunities for *followers* in markets, as Kia has shown in the automobile market and Dell has demonstrated in the TV market. In both cases, these organizations have grown to challenger status in certain market segments. Nevertheless, companies occupying these positions are often vulnerable to attack from their larger and established competitors. Market followers should minimize the risks of such attack through careful use of market segmentation, concentrating only on areas where the company can cope. The key can be to specialize rather than diversify so that resources are not too thinly spread. This means the emphasis is on profitability rather than sales growth. Using R&D as efficiently as possible can also help ensure that resources are used in the most appropriate manner.

In many markets, *nichers* are the most vulnerable competitors. They must avoid competition with other organizations in order to ensure their success, particularly as markets become more mature. This can be achieved by seeking safe market segments, typically in areas where big companies do not believe it is worth competing. Such niches may be secured by specializing on a particular market, customer or marketing mix. However, nichers must avoid becoming over-committed to one small area of the market. This can be achieved by being strong in more than one niche. If there is an aggressive attack on one niche segment, this means that there may be opportunities to switch resources to another. *Fast movers* share the characteristics and approaches of nichers and challengers.

6.3 MONITORING COMPETITORS' STRATEGIES

No matter what the nature of the market, it is of fundamental importance to gain an idea of competitors' strategies. It is not too difficult to review past actions, competitors' product launches, price campaigns, distribution policies, promotional campaigns, press releases; their re-action to the organization's product launches or modifications to sales and marketing programmes, capabilities and apparent plans. Many companies are surprisingly predictable.

As with the marketing environment analysis, managers in an organization often know a lot about their competitors: from chance discussions, press comment, industry gossip, dealer feedback, and the sales force. However, such insights may not be shared with colleagues until it is too late. Review workshops harnessing the knowledge of colleagues can be very revealing, especially when supplemented with external industry observers and analysts.

Those companies routinely devoting resources to assessing competitors examine the SWOTs of rivals, their corporate and target market strategies, bases for competing, decision making culture, track record and previous behaviours, as well as current sales and marketing programmes. The challenge lies in persuading the organization to allocate managerial time and database resource to assessing competitors. With an 'ear to the ground', much marketing intelligence can be gathered about competitors at low cost:

- product and pricing activities;
- dealer and customer service moves;
- major account purchases or account moves;
- investment decisions and plans;
- likely reaction to the organization's moves and marketing plan;
- reactions to changes in the trading environment.

6.4 RECORDING COMPETITIVE POSITIONS AND STRENGTHS ON THE COMPETITIVE POSITIONS PROFORMA

As detailed in Chapter 5, it is important to know what product, sales and marketing attributes customers expect and need. It is also important to know which Key Customer Values (KCVs) each competitor is believed to offer or deliver, and whether in so doing any competitor gains a differential or competitive advantage in the marketplace over its rivals. A *differential advantage* is something a company or its marketing mix has which is desired by the target market, and is not currently readily matched by rival companies or products. The concept builds from the 'unique selling proposition' or USP so popular with sales managers in the 1970s. Knowing which rivals are growing significantly is also crucial, even the smaller ones! This ensures that key competitive challenges are adequately addressed in marketing plans. To help compete effectively, marketers should also be aware of rivals' weaknesses which it may be possible to exploit.

The authors developed the competitive positions proforma in their *Marketing Planning Workbook* in the early 1990s. This succinct approach to capturing competitive insights has proved popular with many leadership teams and marketing directors, and other authors. The approach works by portraying the key threats which competitors pose and thus revealing the organization's own standing in each target market. The completed proforma shows how to compete effectively and acts as a call to action. The marketing programme appearing in the marketing plan must reflect these issues. It should be noted that identified substitute solutions and new entrants may be included as cells in this proforma's columns.

Figure 6.2 provides a suitable summary proforma per segment which:

  (i) aggregates information regarding the competitors and positions occupied within each target market or market segment; by including your organization in the 'league table' the nature of the competitive challenge is starkly revealed;
 (ii) considers the KCVs satisfied by competitors and thereby scopes how well rivals are serving customers;
(iii) examines whether rivals have a differential/competitive advantage that needs to be addressed;
 (iv) identifies competitors' weaknesses that may be exploited, but also the organization's weaknesses which may be leveraged by rivals;
  (v) shows which competitors are gaining market share and which are moving up the 'league table' when the analysis is repeated some months later.

The authors' textbook website for their title *Marketing: Concepts and Strategies* provides further explanation for conducting an analysis of competitors and using the Dibb/Simkin Competitive Positions Proforma. Access this at www.dibbmarketing.com, select the 'Student Section' in the menu, then *Practitioners' Use of Key Analytical Tools*. From the sub-menu, select 'Using the Dibb/Simkin Competitive Positions Proforma to Assess Competitors'. Figure 6.3 presents a second illustrative example of a completed Competitive Positions proforma.

Marketers use the outputs from this analysis to steer their marketing programmes and prioritize where to devote their marketing budgets. Leadership teams of organizations find that using this analysis in conjunction with the DPM approach described in the next chapter provides a great sense of direction for resourcing decisions and strategic planning. Many companies update this analysis every three months. At the very least, the competitive positions proforma should be produced annually in the organization's marketing plan. Progress up the 'league table' or slips down the column are indicative of the effectiveness of the organization's marketing strategy and marketing programmes.

FIGURE 6.2　Competitive positions and differential advantage proforma

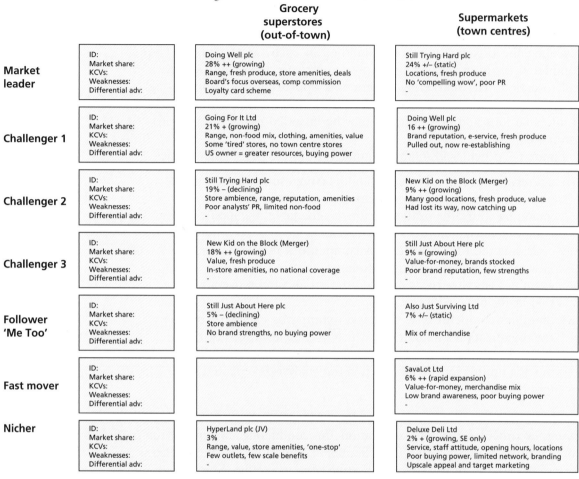

Disguised example, UK grocery retailing by channel to market

	ID:	Grocery superstores (out-of-town)	Supermarkets (town centres)
Market leader	Market share: KCVs: Weaknesses: Differential adv:	Doing Well plc 28% ++ (growing) Range, fresh produce, store amenities, deals Board's focus overseas, comp commission Loyalty card scheme	Still Trying Hard plc 24% +/– (static) Locations, fresh produce No 'compelling wow', poor PR -
Challenger 1	ID: Market share: KCVs: Weaknesses: Differential adv:	Going For It Ltd 21% + (growing) Range, non-food mix, clothing, amenities, value Some 'tired' stores, no town centre stores US owner = greater resources, buying power	Doing Well plc 16 ++ (growing) Brand reputation, e-service, fresh produce Pulled out, now re-establishing -
Challenger 2	ID: Market share: KCVs: Weaknesses: Differential adv:	Still Trying Hard plc 19% – (declining) Store ambience, range, reputation, amenities Poor analysts' PR, limited non-food -	New Kid on the Block (Merger) 9% ++ (growing) Many good locations, fresh produce, value Had lost its way, now catching up
Challenger 3	ID: Market share: KCVs: Weaknesses: Differential adv:	New Kid on the Block (Merger) 18% ++ (growing) Value, fresh produce In-store amenities, no national coverage -	Still Just About Here plc 9% = (growing) Value-for-money, brands stocked Poor brand reputation, few strengths
Follower 'Me Too'	ID: Market share: KCVs: Weaknesses: Differential adv:	Still Just About Here plc 5% – (declining) Store ambience No brand strengths, no buying power -	Also Just Surviving Ltd 7% +/– (static) Mix of merchandise -
Fast mover	ID: Market share: KCVs: Weaknesses: Differential adv:		SavaLot Ltd 6% ++ (rapid expansion) Value-for-money, merchandise mix Low brand awareness, poor buying power -
Nicher	ID: Market share: KCVs: Weaknesses: Differential adv:	HyperLand plc (JV) 3% Range, value, store amenities, 'one-stop' Few outlets, few scale benefits -	Deluxe Deli Ltd 2% + (growing, SE only) Service, staff attitude, opening hours, locations Poor buying power, limited network, branding Upscale appeal and target marketing

- Record the competitive positions separately for each target market/segment, using a column for each
- The KCVs on this chart are those KCVs that each competitor is able to match/serve
- Most companies do not have a DA (differential advantage), so this slot may be left blank for many companies' positions
- If competitors' market shares are known, enter them in the column. Often such data are not known. There is *no* need to list actual %s for market share changes, current year versus last year. Key to market share entries: ++ large market share increase; + small market share increase; – small market share decline; –– large market share decline

© Sally Dibb & Lyndon Simkin

FIGURE 6.3 Example of the competitive positions proforma

Mars – chocolate confectionery

Competitive positions	Chocolate confectionery high volume, low cost
Market leader Market share move: KCVs offered: Weaknesses: Any DA:	**Mars** 15.7% +/- Variety, consistency Old brands, not innovative Privately owned, strength of brand
Challenger 1 Market share move: KCVs offered: Weaknesses: Any DA:	**Nestle** 15.4 - Price, product design Misreading consumer needs / wants Huge corporation
Challenger 2 Market share move: KCVs offered: Weaknesses: Any DA:	**Hersheys** 10.2 + Variety, availability, innovative North America centric Local brand, iconic
Challenger 3 Market share move: KCVs offered: Weaknesses: Any DA:	**Kraft** 7.8 ++ Position in market (gift) Small product range Distribution, uniqueness
Challenger 4 Market share move: KCVs offered: Weaknesses: Any DA:	**Cadburys** 7.1% + Simple, block chocolate Not global brand scale Brand (heritage)
Market Nicher Market share move: KCVs offered: Weaknesses: Any DA:	**Ferrero Roche** 7.1 + Exclusivity, associations with status Limited range, seasonal Unique products and packaging
Market Nicher Market share move: KCVs offered: Weaknesses: Any DA:	**Lindt** 3.1 ++ High quality, range of products More expensive Swiss tradition

[Based on trade research]

SUMMARY

This chapter has built an overview of the competitive arena in which organizations operate. The impact of an organization's marketing strategy is shaped by the actions of various competitive players and the way in which each strives to match key customer values. It is important to understand how competitors will react to the company's target market strategy and associated marketing plan programmes; not only like-for-like rivals, but substitute providers and possible new entrants.

No company can operate in isolation of its competitors' moves and it is vital to anticipate their reactions. Many companies behave in a surprisingly 'predictable' manner. Examining their recent past and marketing initiatives should give a reasonable clue to their forthcoming moves and their reaction to the organization's planned marketing programmes. It should be possible to 'second guess' how rivals will behave. It is also important to realize which competitors are good or bad at matching target customers' needs, as this will reveal rivals' strengths and weaknesses in terms of satisfying customers, possibly presenting the company with opportunities or some threats. Competitors with a differential advantage pose a significant threat and must be combated. Standings over time will alter so the assessment of competitors must be ongoing.

7

The strength of the portfolio and future directions

The final two essential background marketing analyses of the ASP process concern the organization's products. It is essential to have products or services which assist in maximizing opportunities and which are in line with key customer needs. No company has a portfolio of totally successful products: some will be on the decline if not already dying, some will still have to realize their potential, while a few will be the company's current cash cows. Recognizing which products are the organization's 'bread and butter', helps identify where nurturing is required and pinpoints those which are a drain on resources. This chapter presents the directional policy matrix approach to managing the product portfolio. The tool's use of a balanced set of attractiveness criteria is productive in also determining which opportunities and which target markets or market segments to select.

The chapter also examines the product life cycle concept, which holds that all products have a life, passing from birth, into growth, to maturity and ultimately into decline. Knowing where the market is and the status of the organization's products versus rivals can be revealing. This can help with tricky decisions about when to withdraw from markets or kill off problem products and brands, freeing resources which can be more productively focused on emerging opportunities. These approaches help to address the following issues:

- assessing the merits of the product portfolio;
- selecting between opportunities and target markets;
- understanding the product life cycle.

7.1 THE BALANCED PORTFOLIO

7.1.1 The directional policy matrix approach to assessing business strength and market attractiveness

Part Two of *Marketing Planning* has examined the core background analyses which lead to the successful understanding of a market. The final analyses concern the health of the existing product portfolio, with the aim of ensuring there is a balanced portfolio of products and markets. The tools also assist in opportunity selection and the creation of a target market strategy.

The aim of the Market Attractiveness/Business Position Matrix or the Directional Policy Matrix (DPM) is to assess the relative attractiveness of investing in particular areas, so as to determine appropriate strategic planning goals and appropriate funding/human resources. The unit of analysis can be an SBU (strategic business unit), a product group, individual products or brands, target markets or market segments. Typically companies set up SBUs on the basis of core product groups or territories, but for the purposes of this exercise it may be more appropriate to use markets or market segments (perhaps in conjunction with territories, for organizations with international markets).

An organization reviews the performance of each of its SBUs, products or market segments in the context of the organization's overall mix of SBUs, segments and product portfolio. The relative 'health' or potential of each SBU (or product or market) in the context of the overall product portfolio enables the company to decide which SBUs/products/markets to *build* (develop further/increase market share), *maintain* (resources to keep the status quo/current market share), *harvest* (sell-off/pull out of after squeezing the last potential sales), or *divest* (drop more or less immediately).

Most managers intuitively know which products or markets are yesterday's 'has-beens' or tomorrow's 'breadwinners'. Yet managerial impressions are rarely a sufficient basis for such fundamental decision making. Hence, the development of such analytical portfolio planning techniques by the major consultancies (McKinsey and the Boston Consultancy Group) and blue chip companies (such as General Electric or Shell).

7.1.2 Assessing market attractiveness and business strength

(i) Depending on the unit of analysis – SBUs, product groups, products, markets or market segments – the first step is to decide which *variables* are the *most appropriate* for assessing the *market attractiveness*. This is assessed relative to the market as a whole. It is important that a cross-functional set of managers selects the criteria, not just marketers. The selected variables should include some longer-term factors and market-facing factors and not focus simply on current profitability!

(ii) Separately, this selection of criteria is repeated for the *business position*, sometimes called the competitive position or business strength. This dimension is assessed relative to the leading/strongest competitor or relative market share. The chosen variables are typically very industry-specific, focusing on the strengths major players emphasize and for which customers look.

   These decisions are usually based on the informed judgement of management taking into consideration any relevant research information. Generally, it is best not to exceed ten or twelve variables in each list. For example, when assessing market attractiveness, one company manufacturing agricultural equipment uses eight: industry sales, product sales, market share, profitability, competitor intensity, customer retention rate, future growth prospects and ability to create differentiation.

(iii) Once the two lists of variables have been derived for the market attractiveness and business position, the importance of each of the variables relative to the others is decided. An appropriate *weighting* is allocated. The total weighting should add up to 100 for each list. For example, when considering market attractiveness, market share may be seen to be a particularly important factor and be allocated a weighting of 40.

   There are now two agreed lists: attractiveness criteria and business position (or business strength) variables. Each list's variables have been weighted by the management team conducting the assessment. These stages will *not* need repeating in the future: these two lists and their weightings should remain constant over a period of time, to allow changes in the items plotted on the DPM to be assessed. The next stages, (iv) and (v), however, must be repeated each time the DPM is produced.

(iv) Next, give a *score* to each variable which reflects how the particular SBU/product group/product/market/segment (depending on the selected unit of analysis) under consideration shapes up relative to others being assessed. One way to do this is to make $0.0 = low/poor$, $0.5 = medium/average$, and $1.0 = high/good$ for each selected variable. It is possible to use 5 or 7 point scales for scoring, but keeping the scoring simple (e.g. 0, .5 and 1) works perfectly well and is much easier to apply in practice. Then repeat the process for the other SBUs/product groups/products/markets/segments (depending on the chosen level of analysis).

(v) Multiply the weighting by the score to give a *ranking* for each variable. The *sum* of the rankings for each SBU/product group/product/market/segment analysed should then be calculated. This stage will give a total out of 100 for the market attractiveness dimension and a separate total out of 100 for the business position dimension.

(vi) Plot the two totals from (v) for each SBU/product group/product/market/segment position on the matrix using a circle. The diameter of the circle usually reflects the sales volume or

proportion of total company income from the SBU/product group/
product/market/segment. If the market size is known, an area of
the circle can be shaded to show the market share (as in Figure
7.1). This is useful, otherwise small circles plotted to the bottom
right of the DPM might be disinvested even though the
organization already enjoys dominant market share with any
capital investment paid back long ago.

7.1.3 Worked example of the DPM

The boxes shown in Tables 7.1 and 7.2 are as the analysis would work
for an individual SBU, product group, product, market or market segment being assessed for the DPM. In this mocked-up example, the
selected unit of analysis has achieved a market attractiveness total of
62.5 and a business position total of 82.5. These values would be plotted on the DPM, with its axes scaled at 1–100 each.

Market attractiveness

TABLE 7.1   Example DPM analysis for an individual SBU – market attractiveness

Variable	Agreed weighting	Agreed scoring	Final ranking
Industry sales	5	0	0
Product sales	10	0.5	5
Market share	25	0.5	12.5
Profitability	25	1	25
Competitor intensity	10	0.5	5
Customer retention rate	10	0.5	5
Future growth prospects	10	1	10
Ability to create differentiation	5	0	0
			62.5

Business position/competitive position

TABLE 7.2   Example DPM analysis for an individual SBU – business position

Variable	Agreed weighting	Agreed scoring	Final ranking
Product quality	25	1	25
New technology	5	0.5	2.5
Sales force coverage	15	0.5	7.5
Service back-up	15	0.5	7.5
Manufacturing skills	20	1	20
Distribution proficiency	20	1	20
			82.5

7.1.4 Interpreting the DPM

Figure 7.1 shows an example of a completed matrix and Figure 7.2 the outline generic strategies to follow. In general, those SBUs/product groups/products/markets/segments appearing in the top left of the chart can be deemed as the 'star' products or markets. Those SBUs/product groups/products/markets/segments (depending on the selected level of analysis) which appear in the bottom left area of the chart, will typically be the 'cash cows' for the company (those products on which the company depends for the bulk of its income/cash generation).

SBUs/product groups/products/market/segments floating around in the centre and top right segment of the chart tend to be those for which the future is uncertain (in other words over which there is a question mark). For these, further analysis and scenario planning are required so that a decision can be made on whether to cut losses and cease production or to put full marketing/distributor resources behind a major push.

SBUs/product groups/products/markets/segments which are located in the bottom right segment of the chart are the real 'dogs' in the portfolio, with very little potential and probably already making losses. These 'dog' products should be dropped immediately or in the very near future – unless the organization already enjoys dominant market share at low marketing cost, with all capital investments already long paid back, or if withdrawal from this area might expose the organization to attack from a competitor who is able to address this area and then build on its sales in order to attack more strongly elsewhere.

7.1.5 Levels of analysis

Commonly, companies tend to undertake this type of analysis first at the product group level, then by pulling together all product groups,

FIGURE 7.1 Example of a completed DPM

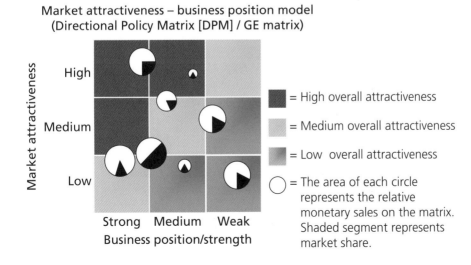

Market attractiveness – business position model
(Directional Policy Matrix [DPM] / GE matrix)

F I G U R E   7 . 2   Strategy implications from DPM positions

	High	Business position/strengths	Low
High	**Highly desirable/protect** – Invest for growth – Maintain strengths – Defend this market or opportunity	**Significant potential** – A challenge for senior managers to get right – Highly attractive – Strengths need selectively building and weaknesses addressing	**Caution/Selectivity** – Highly attractive but limited/poor capabilities – Try to minimize weaknesses with low investment – Be prepared to withdraw
Market attractiveness	**Caution/Selectivity** – Strong capabilities, but only average attractiveness – Focus on key segments – Increase productivity – Address competitors' moves	**Manage for £s** – Defend existing activity – Focus on desirable segments with low risk – Seek to improve strengths at low cost	**Harvest/Withdraw** – Minimize expenditure and rationalize operations – Only expand with low investment – Resources might be better used elsewhere
Low	**Protect/Invest elsewhere** – Manage for current earnings to leverage strong capabilities – Focus on best segments – Spend in more attractive areas/opportunities	**Take the money** – Defend position but only in key segments – Upgrade products – Keep investment minimal – Put resources elsewhere	**Kill off/Divest** – Cut fixed costs – Avoid any investment here – Withdraw so as to use efforts where more useful – Stop doing this!

for the company as a whole, segment by segment. The analysis can, however, be focused on many levels, such as company-wide for all individual products, for certain product groups/SBUs, for individual products, for specific market segments, separate countries, certain dealer types or for any permutation. The DPM is particularly useful in deciding which market segments to target: see Section 8.3.

Clearly, however, the concept is intended to look at a company's overall performance and too narrow a focus may detract from the technique's worth. The 'common' approach is for the Marketing Director to focus on the SBU level for all segments, with individual Marketing Managers examining the portfolio at the product level.

7.1.6 Recording the portfolio analysis

The variables which make a market attractive need to be determined, weighted, scored and ranked, see Figures 7.1 and 7.2. Similarly, the variables which the organization feels affect the business position must be agreed. A cross-hierarchical and cross-functional management team should – either by e-poll or in a workshop – suggest variables, select those variables to use in the DPM, agree weightings and then 'judge'

FIGURE 7.3   Information required for the DPM analysis

Market attractiveness			
Variables	Weightings	Scores	Ranking/totals

Business strength/Competitive position			
Variables	Weightings	Scores	Ranking/totals

- Select the variables felt to be most important. Complete the columns
- This information now needs to be plotted on a graph, Figure 7.4, as in Figure 7.1

What are the Implications from this analysis?

each unit of analysis in the scoring part of producing the DPM. The team should meet to discuss the implications from the resulting DPM plot. Figure 7.3 presents a grid for pulling this information together, while Figure 7.4 is the DPM outline.

The authors' textbook website for their title *Marketing: Concepts and Strategies* provides further explanation for conducting a DPM analysis, with worked examples. Access this at www.dibbmarketing.com, select the 'Student Section' in the menu, then *Practitioners' Use of Key Analytical Tools*. From the sub-menu, select 'Producing a Directional Policy Matrix in Portfolio Analysis'.

7.2 THE PRODUCT LIFE CYCLE

Marketers often consider that products or services have a 'life cycle', similar to people. Products are born (created) and introduced into the market. There is a growth period as consumer interest and sales

FIGURE 7.4 The DPM proforma

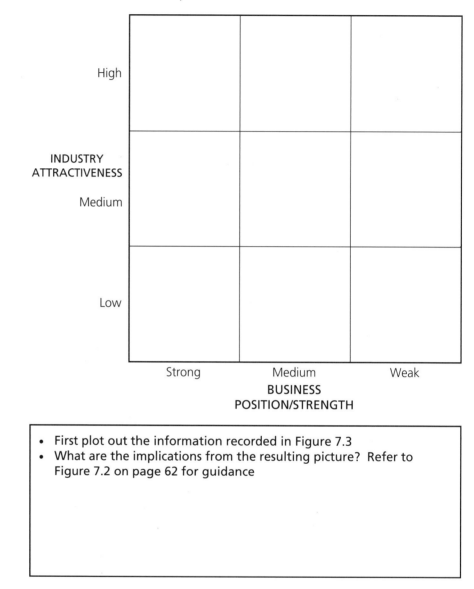

- First plot out the information recorded in Figure 7.3
- What are the implications from the resulting picture? Refer to Figure 7.2 on page 62 for guidance

increase. Eventually, products lose their appeal and sales decline, effectively 'killing off' the product. For poor products there may be no growth period, with death occurring soon after the product's birth or launch. This product life cycle (PLC) can be represented by a sales growth curve and industry profit graph, see Figure 7.5.

There is a trend towards shorter life cycles, led by fast moving customer requirements and competitive activity, making it difficult for some companies to recover NPD and R&D costs during the model's life cycle.

FIGURE 7.5 The product life cycle (PLC)

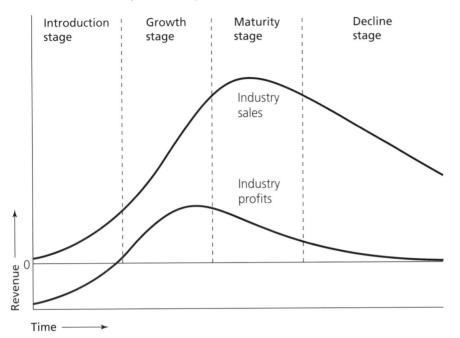

Source: S. Dibb, L. Simkin, O. C. Ferrell and W. Pride, *Marketing: Concepts and Strategies*, Fifth edition. Copyright © 2006 Houghton Mifflin Company. Used with permission.

7.2.1 Introduction stage

It is estimated that between 33 per cent and 90 per cent of all new products fail. During the introduction stage, buyers need to be made aware of the product and their direct interest kindled. Development and marketing costs will be high. Prices are often high, but product development and marketing costs can result in negative profits.

The marketer can opt for rapid or slow skimming, rapid or slow penetration. Under rapid skimming, the product is introduced with a high price and high sales and advertising support, with the intention of achieving the greatest possible revenue per unit sold. This is an attractive proposition if customers seem eager to buy. With slow skimming, the sale price is high, but promotional support is less. Revenue is required, but costs must be kept down. This is a useful approach when the market size is expected to be small, the potential buyers are eager and competition is minimal.

For rapid penetration, there is high spending on promotion, but the price is relatively low: the aim is to achieve a fast take-off and large market share. This is an appropriate way forward if the market is large, unaware of the product, if competition is likely and if buyers are price sensitive. For slow penetration, there is low price with low promotional support to gain rapid market acceptance at low cost to the company.

7.2.2 Growth

During this stage there is a rapid increase in sales. Profits can be seen to peak – as manufacturing and marketing costs are spread across more sales – and then profits decline as more competitors enter the booming market to 'ride on the back' of those companies which have created the market. Price cutting can occur as competition increases.

The strategy in the growth stage aims to maintain growth as long as possible through improving product quality, adding new features, moving into additional market segments, using new distribution channels, altering promotion or revising prices. These approaches can improve a company's competitive position, but all have cost implications. The organization strives, though, for longer term gains.

7.2.3 Maturity

Throughout maturity, competition intensifies. Competitors are forced to offer improved products with shrewder marketing programmes. Sales peak, then level off, revealing the plateau in the PLC. Companies engage in increased promotional activity to stave off impending decline. Almost inevitably, profits decline as competition intensifies, more products are added to ranges and promotional costs rise.

The maturity stage lasts longer than the others, so it is often sub-divided into growth maturity, stable maturity and decaying maturity. The slow down in sales leads to over capacity and declining profits. Competition intensifies with price cutting and heavy advertising. Some weaker competitors drop out of the market. For the more entrenched companies, the task is to attain a distinct differential or competitive advantage.

Surviving companies opt for one or a mixture of three approaches:

(a) Market modification involves converting non-users, entering new segments or winning market share from competitors. Sometimes volumes can be increased by finding new uses for the product or by encouraging more frequent purchase.
(b) Product modification, with new features or quality improvements to attract more usage or new users.
(c) Marketing mix modification to stimulate sales by manipulating pricing, promotion, service or distribution.

7.2.4 Decline

Eventually sales fall rapidly. This can be because of changing customer tastes, competing substitute products, social concerns, legislation, media coverage or corporate policies. Companies face severe competition coupled with declining revenues. Product portfolios will require rationalization and, at some point, the decision may be made to divest from the market entirely.

Strategies are relatively few: weak products must be identified and withdrawn from the market. Market share, sales, profits and contributions will make this decision reasonably obvious, if far from palatable. When the product is dropped, the company must decide whether to sell it on to a different supplier, transfer it over or kill it off completely. Decisions must also be made as to whether the product should be phased out quickly or slowly.

7.2.5 The PLC in marketing planning

The PLC is a useful concept in planning, as a control mechanism for marketing activities, and in sales forecasting. In the context of marketing planning, the PLC helps to identify the main challenges facing each product. There will be slightly different PLC positions for a product sold to more than one target market in each market. It is important to understand the PLC position, product by product, market by market, and to incorporate the strategic implications in the development of marketing strategies (as explored in the next few chapters) and marketing programmes for implementation. Figure 7.6 enables the implications from the PLC analysis to be considered and addressed in the marketing plan.

FIGURE 7.6 The stages of the PLC

Segment and product	PLC stage	Implications
• For each product in each segment indicate the stage in the PLC reached – in column 2 • In column 3, suggest the more obvious strategic implications for each product		

SUMMARY

The directional policy matrix (DPM) can be used to assess the health of the organization in terms of the balance of the product portfolio and target markets. By reviewing the performance of each product or product group, decisions can be made about areas in which to invest. If markets or market segments are assessed using the DPM, more objective decisions are possible concerning which to prioritize in the target market strategy. With the knowledge of customers' needs and of competitors' ability to match these, the product portfolio can be managed within the marketing planning initiative to good effect. Cash draining areas can be identified so that, if necessary, a disinvestment strategy can also be followed. The DPM is useful for examining the health of the current portfolio of products as well as for longer term planning in selecting attractive markets of the future. The product life cycle (PLC) concept is similarly useful for contributing to the diagnosis of problem areas and future moves. Both concepts assist in identifying probable declines for the company and in balancing desired marketing programme spends against likely returns. They assist in realigning resources to growth opportunities and the most attractive markets.

8

Marketing strategy

There are four key components to the marketing strategy section of marketing planning: the selection of opportunities to pursue, the determination of target market segments, the basis on which to compete in each target market, and finally the desired brand positioning in the minds of the targeted customers versus competitors. These strategic decisions need to be in the context of the organization's mission statement, discussed first in this chapter.

It is essential that the recommended marketing strategy within the marketing plan fully reflects the information and market situation presented by the marketing analyses outlined in the previous chapters. It is unrealistic to believe that pre-existing marketing strategy choices will suffice in the light of the updated marketing intelligence. This chapter will help the marketer to:

- agree priorities to pursue;
- select a target market strategy;
- consider the basis for competing effectively;
- produce the desired brand positioning.

8.1 MISSION STATEMENT AND OPPORTUNITIES

Most organizations have a stated mission statement summing up their sense of purpose. If there is not one already defined, now is a good time to define it, given the knowledge of the organization and its standing revealed in the core marketing analyses. Where a mission statement does exist, it is likely to have been developed by senior management not as aware of core trends and issues identified by the analysis of the marketplace. Some modification and updating will probably be needed.

Nevertheless, the stated sense of purpose in the organization's mission statement must be incorporated in the marketing function's thinking as strategies are finalized within marketing planning. The recommended strategies, and ultimately the associated marketing programmes for implementation, must relate to the organization's stated purpose. Equally, the opportunities selected to pursue should sit comfortably with the mission statement.

Mission statements tend to fall into one of several categories. First, there are very broad statements typically found in annual reports:

> *This company strives for perfection in its product development, customer service and commitment to the natural environment.*
> *The company will become the leading supplier of detergents in Europe through acquisition and prudent use of resources.*

Such 'motherhood' statements may keep the media and shareholders happy, but otherwise are relatively meaningless in terms of marketing actions.

The second category of mission statements comprise meaningful statements unique to the organization which impact on the behaviour of all executives and personnel, affecting sales and marketing decisions.

A third category contains a functional statement derived by the marketing function and appropriate to a business unit or to one product group. For example, JCB dominates the European market for construction equipment, but in large crawler excavators it is a relatively minor player. The mission for this product group is to take leadership in the UK market, make significant, specified in-roads into certain other territories, while establishing a presence, no matter how small, in other stated territories in Europe. This is a very different situation from that faced by the company's other product groups, many of which dominate Europe.

The mission statement should include, in less than one page:

- *Stated role*: profit (contribution), service, opportunities sought; immediate priorities and medium-term goals.

- *Business definition*: in terms of customer needs, benefits provided – not only the products produced.

- *Company strengths, advantages, marketing assets*: qualities which create the foundation for the organization's fortunes and ability to service markets.

An important aspect of marketing planning is opportunity identification and then selection. As explored in Chapters 3 and 4, the analysis of the marketing environment and the SWOT analysis both lead to the identification of opportunities but, as explained in Chapters 5 and 6, so do the analyses of customers' buying behaviour and competitors' positions. The resulting set of possible opportunities and pursuits should be graded. No organization has the resources or commitment to tackle everything. The DPM market attractiveness criteria highlighted in

Chapter 7 are well suited to this judging of which ideas are worthy of developing into full business cases and cost–benefit analyses. Only the emerging opportunities which rank above average on the DPM attractiveness axis vis-à-vis existing activities should be included in the organization's marketing plan.

8.2 TARGET MARKETS

Marketing plans ultimately centre on marketing programmes based on the marketing mix. Such plans must exist to implement a clear target market strategy and emphasize any advantages over competitors. Without detailed implementation plans, senior management is unlikely to authorize the required marketing budgets.

Having analysed the market, the organization must turn its improved understanding of the market's activities and requirements into a clear strategy statement. This involves identifying the markets to target, any differential advantages for the company's products or services, and the required product or service positionings.

8.2.1 Market segmentation

A proper understanding of the varying needs and requirements of different customers is fundamental to the principles of marketing. Although companies may recognize the breadth of such needs, it is unrealistic to customize products to suit each individual, unless concentrating on a niche market. Moving away from mass marketing or, at the other extreme, bespoke customized services, towards a market segmentation approach where the focus is on a particular group (or groups) of customers, is an increasingly popular way of dealing with this diversity of needs. Furthermore, by adopting a different basis to its segmentation than that used by rivals, an organization can gain an edge over competitors in servicing targeted customers' needs. A market segment contains similarly behaving like-minded business customers or consumers. Segmentation is the process of identifying these homogeneous groups, selecting which to target and how best to engage with these target markets.

Many companies believe that marketing success is linked to how effectively their customer base is segmented. Market segmentation allows companies to go some of the way towards satisfying diverse customer needs while maintaining certain scale economies. The process begins by grouping together customers with similar requirements and buying characteristics. Next, the organization can select the group(s) on which to target its sales, marketing and brands. A marketing programme can then be designed to cater for the specific requirements and characteristics of the targeted group(s) or segment(s) of customers. This marketing programme will aim to position the product, brand or service directly at the targeted consumers. Such positioning will take into consideration the offerings of competing organizations within the same segment.

The benefits which a market segmentation approach offers are many and varied. These benefits include a better understanding of customer needs and wants, which can lead to more carefully attuned and effective marketing programmes; greater insight into the competitive situation, which assists in the identification and maintenance of a differential advantage, and more effective resource allocation. Rarely is it realistic to target 100 percent of a market, so focusing on certain segments allows organizations to make efficient use of their resources.

The potential benefits offered by market segmentation can help companies to take advantage of marketing opportunities which might otherwise be missed. These opportunities can be related to activities in new or existing product markets as outlined by Ansoff:

- *Market penetration* allows companies to increase their percentage of sales in existing markets by taking sales from competitors. For example, this can be achieved by an aggressive and well-targeted promotional campaign or bespoke one-off customer support activities such as a free processing of sample customer data, or free demonstrations of facilities.

- *Product development* involves offering new or improved products to current markets, through the expansion of the product range. Product development may be quite minor, such as extending the flexibility or colour options of a product, or quite major such as the development of a totally new line. The development of a product may be in-house or in conjunction with external companies.

- *Market development* involves the sale of existing products to new markets, typically by finding new applications.

- *Diversification* is about seeking opportunities in new markets by offering new products.

There are implications here from the product life cycle stage reached (see Section 7.2).

8.2.2 The segmentation process

Any market segmentation consists of three distinct stages. It is important to fully understand these stages before making any major decisions about how different markets should be segmented. The illustration below demonstrates the relationship between the key stages.

Segmentation
- Consider different variables for segmenting the market from those currently used.

- Look at the profile of the emerging (new and existing) segments.
- Check the validity of the segments.

Targeting
- Decide on an appropriate targeting strategy.
- Consider which and how many segments should be targeted.
- Decide which are the priority target segments.

Positioning
- In each segment, understand customer perceptions of all key brands.
- Position the organization's products in the mind of the customers and distributors/dealers in the targeted segment against rivals' products and brands.
- Design an appropriate marketing mix which conveys this desired positioning to the targeted customers.

Put simply, the underlying principle of the three stages is that 'similar' customers can be grouped. For example, an audience of 100 managers asked about their favourite car model might give 100 different responses. However, some of the responses might refer to sports cars, others to 4-wheel-drive, off-road vehicles, while a further group could be centred on executive cars. In situations where such 'similar' consumers can be collected into large enough groups, there is obvious potential for companies wishing to target such *segments*. The InterContinental Hotels Case Study in Chapter 17 illustrates how this company has created separate brands and product concepts in order to address its selected target market segments.

8.2.3 Carrying out segmentation

Carrying out segmentation, the stage where customers are aggregated into groups, involves two basic steps:

(i) Segmentation variables (also called *base variables*) are used to group together customers who demonstrate similar product requirements and buying behaviour. When choosing appropriate segmentation bases it is necessary to select those which clearly distinguish between different product requirements and behaviours.

Probably the most popular industrial or business-to-business segmentation bases include:

- geographic location;
- type of organization;
- trade category;
- customer size/characteristics;

- customers' business sectors;
- product-related features:
  - purchase behaviour,
  - purchase occasion,
  - benefits sought from having the product,
  - consumption behaviour,
  - attitude to product/service.

Bear in mind that choosing segmentation bases is a fairly subjective process, so it is rarely possible to categorically assert that there is *one* best way to segment a particular market.

In consumer markets, companies used to break down customers into groups by income, age and social class. Increasingly, consumer marketers look to additional information, such as customers' perceptions of the benefits attained from purchasing a product, their usage behaviour, and motivation. Advances in information technology and the ability of organizations to capture and manage customer data are resulting in more complex segmentation schemes using more variables than in the past. Figure 8.1 summarizes popular segmentation bases in consumer markets.

For a more detailed examination of how to produce segments, with worked examples, readers should refer to *Market Segmentation Success: Making It Happen!*, by Sally Dibb and Lyndon Simkin, New York: The Haworth Press, 2008.

(ii) Once segments have been identified using one or a combination of the base variables above, as much as possible must be done to understand the characteristics of the customers in those segments. This understanding will make it easier for the marketer to design a marketing programme which will appeal to the segment targeted. Building up a fuller picture of the segments is called *profiling* and uses *descriptor variables*. Descriptors can include variables relating to customer characteristics or product-related behavioural variables. In fact, the more extensive the picture, the better.

Sometimes people find the distinction between *base* and *descriptor variables* confusing. Just remember that *base* variables are used first to allocate customers to segments while *descriptors* help later in building up a profile of segment membership.

8.2.4 Essential qualities for effective segments

As has been stated, there is rarely one 'right' way to segment a market, but there are some criteria which can help to decide on the robustness of a particular approach. Before implementing a segmentation scheme, check that the segments satisfy the following conditions:

- *Measurable*: it must be possible to delimit, measure and assess the segments for market potential.

FIGURE 8.1   Segmentation bases in consumer markets

___

Basic customer characteristics

Owing to the ease with which such information can be obtained, the use of these variables is widespread

- Demographics

  Age   *Sex*
  Family   *Marital status*
  Race   *Religion*
  Family Life cycle

- Socio-Economics

  Income   *Occupation*
  Education   *Social class*

- Geographic location

  Country   *Region*
  Type of urban area   *Urban/rural*
  Type of housing

- Personality, motives and lifestyle

  Consumer's personality
  Motives for purchasing/consuming
  Consumer's lifestyle and aspirations

Product related behavioural characteristics

- Purchase behaviour

  Brand loyalty versus triggers for switching

- Purchase occasion

  Novelty   *Frequency*
  Event   *Dealer location*

- Benefits sought

  The benefits sought by the consumer from purchasing, consuming, having the product or service

- Consumption behaviour and user status

  Heavy users versus light and non-users

- Attitude to product/service

  Different customers' perceptions
  Consumers' communication

___

- *Substantial*: in order to warrant marketing activity, the identified segment must be large enough to be viable and therefore worthwhile targeting with products/services. Separate organizations will have different views as to viable size: Toyota versus Morgan Cars, for example.

- *Accessible*: having identified a market segment, and checked its potential viability, the marketer must be able to action a marketing programme with a finely developed marketing mix for targeted customers. Sometimes the similarities between customers are not sufficient to implement full marketing programmes.
- *Stable*: there must be an assessment of a segment's short-, medium- and long-term viability, particularly in the light of competitor and marketing environment changes. Segments rarely remain the same over time, so it is necessary to weigh up the extent and impact of likely changes.
- *Useful*: the resulting solution must be transparently obvious to sales and marketing personnel within the organization and assist in more readily engaging with business customers or consumers within the targeted segments.

8.3 TARGETING

Once segments have been identified, decisions about how many and which customer groups to target must be made. The options include:

- *Mass marketing strategy*: offering one product concept and marketing mix to most of the market, across many market segments. Although scale economies can be achieved, there is the risk that few customers will be adequately satisfied.
- *Single segment strategy*: concentrating on a single segment with one product concept and marketing mix. This is relatively cheap in resources, but very risky if the segment should fail or aggressive competitors subsequently attack this segment.
- *Multi-segment strategy*: targeting a different product concept and marketing mix at each of a number of segments. Although this approach can spread the risk of being over-committed in one area, it can be extremely resource hungry. This is the most common approach in most organizations, but within a specific profit centre it would normally be better to focus on just one or two segments. Entries into other areas could be undertaken on an *ad hoc* basis, typically to support other profit centre marketing approaches.

Which target market strategy a company adopts will depend on a host of market, product and competitive factors. Each of these must be carefully considered before a decision is made about segments to be targeted. Before making a commitment to any segment it is essential to consider the following issues:

- *Existing market share/market homogeneity*. How similar is the market to current areas of activity and does the organization have market share or brand awareness in related areas on which it can build?

- *Product homogeneity*. Does the organization have relevant expertise on which to build in a related product field, with associated economies of scope?
- *Nature of competitive environment*. What is the level of competition in the market and how is this changing over time?
- *Customer needs*. How extreme/easy to satisfy are customer requirements?
- *Segment size, structure and future potential*. How big is the segment or market, how is it made up and how is it likely to develop in the future?
- *Company resources*. Does the organization have the resources to target the segment under consideration?

Taking a balanced view of these factors helps companies make decisions about the viability of particular segments and ensures that resources are appropriately targeted.

The DPM (directional policy matrix described in Chapter 7) can assist in identifying attractive markets in which the organization has strengths for prioritizing target segments. Each segment should be rated in terms of market attractiveness and business position, then located on a DPM grid as in Figure 7.1. Those segments towards the centre and top left of the grid should be target segment priorities (see Figure 7.2). The DPM is a particularly useful tool in target market selection, even though it was not originally developed for such purposes. In recent years, many organizations have selected a balanced set of market attractiveness and business position criteria in order to utilize the DPM in target market decision making. An example of using the DPM in this way may be found at www.dibbmarketing.com, by selecting the 'Student Section' in the menu, then *Practitioners' Use of Key Analytical Tools*. From the sub-menu, select 'Producing a Directional Policy Matrix in Portfolio Analysis'.

Figure 8.2 provides a summary for the determination of target markets for each opportunity to be pursued.

8.4 BASIS FOR COMPETING: DIFFERENTIAL ADVANTAGE

A basis for competing hinges on successfully identifying a differential advantage (DA) or competitive edge. Without one, success in the marketplace is impossible over the longer term and the organization will be highly vulnerable to competitors' moves. Trading is likely to be purely on the basis of price, and in such circumstances any company eventually fails. With a differential advantage, marketing programmes can emphasize the unique strength or advantage. Competitors do not just have to

FIGURE 8.2 Determination of target markets

Market segment name (in order of priority)	Characteristics of market	Opportunity: why chosen as a target priority?	Existing product/ service offered

- List target markets in order of importance (rank)
- State why each market is important
- Summarize the products offered to each market

catch up, but monumental efforts are then required if they are to ever overtake.

A differential advantage is something the organization or one of its products has, which is highly desired by the target market and is not currently readily matched by rival companies or products. It is a unique aspect of the marketing mix not offered by rivals but sought after by targeted customers.

Toyota in press advertisements stresses the capabilities and friendliness of its dealers; BP its green credentials; Chanel the eminence of its brands and fragrances; the AA its coverage and friendly ability to help; 3M its innovative creativity; DHL its speed and reliability; Duracell the longevity of its cells; Honda the innovation behind the brand's products; BA Club Europe the added service, comfort and convenience; JCB the reassurance in its brand; easyJet the value for money of its low-cost flights; BMW the driving experience for owners.

8.4.1 Steps in determining a differential advantage

Addressing the following questions helps in the determination of a differential advantage:

   (i) What segments are there in the market?
  (ii) What product and service attributes are desired and demanded by each segment or customer group?
 (iii) Which of these attributes does the organization offer?
 (iv) What do the organization's competitors offer? What are their genuine strengths (as perceived by the marketplace)?
  (v) Where are the gaps between customer expectations and competitors' offers?

(vi) Are any of these gaps matched by the organization, its products/services or marketing mix? If so, these are differential advantages (DAs).

(vii) Can any of these advantages for the organization be emphasized through sales and marketing programmes?

(viii) How sustainable are these advantages for the organization? How easily can competitors catch up? How well can the organization defend these advantages?

(ix) If there are no current advantages for the organization, given the gaps identified between competitors' offerings and customer expectations, what needs to be developed by the organization?

(x) In order to maximize any existing or potential advantages, what changes must the organization make to its R&D, engineering, sales and marketing?

If there is a differential advantage, the marketing plan's actions must seek to exploit this edge over rivals and communicate it effectively internally and externally.

8.4.2 Givens versus advantages

Managers often identify apparent advantages which frequently are no more than just strengths. Competitive prices, consistent quality, technical performance, delivery, brand credibility, technical support may be keen, but in reality may be matched or bettered by at least some of the strongest competitors. A strength is not a differential advantage or competitive edge if it is matched by rivals.

Similarly, an advantage or strength is not really the basis for competing in a market if in reality it is a 'given': something expected and taken for granted by customers and dealers. Keen price, delivery on time and product quality are a few examples of attributes customers assume to be there and which are taken for granted. A differential advantage has to go further; it must genuinely appeal to customers and be ahead of the competition's offerings.

A workshop for a leading manufacturer of paints identified these bases for competing differential advantages. Subsequent work showed these attributes to be 'givens' – aspects either taken for granted by customers or matched by rivals. These issues had once put this manufacturer well ahead of its rivals, but they had all caught up and the customers had become educated by all players to expect these:

● competitive price;
● consistent quality;
● technical performance;
● delivery;
● credibility;
● technical support.

Unfortunately, managers often fail to recognize that life moves on and previous advantages have been superseded by rivals' offerings. Another common mistake is to benchmark the company's new product against its old one, inevitably identifying numerous advantages in the new product. It is important to remember that while targeted customers might compare the organization's new product with its old one, they will also be judging the new product against competitors' products. As a result, many of the stated advantages will disappear as the organization's new product may not be superior to competitors' products.

8.4.3 Assessing differential advantages

For each segment it is important to determine what product/service/marketing/brand attributes are required or expected by these customers and dealers. The next step is to decide which of these attributes is (or could be) offered by the organization and whether any of these attributes are offered by leading competitors. If they are not, they may form the basis for a differential advantage or competitive edge for the organization. These attributes wanted by target customers, provided by the company and not matched by leading rivals, must be capable of seeming attractive to distributors and to customers; they must be suitable to form the core of sales and marketing programmes, otherwise they are not really the basis for competing. Figure 8.3 provides a suitable summary for this analysis.

FIGURE 8.3   Identification of Differential Advantages (DAs)

Segment name	Identified advantages (strengths) for the business over rivals	Are advantages a sufficient basis for a differential advantage?
1		
2		
3		
4		
5		
6		
7		
8		

- Record any DAs held by the organization over rivals
- Remember a strength is only a possible DA if target customers desire it and rivals do not offer it
- Consider that to be sufficient for a DA, the strength must be cost effective and in the short term, defensible

8.5 BRAND AND PRODUCT POSITIONINGS

Managers' views are important, but there is no substitute for identifying how *customers* and *distributors* perceive brands and products versus the strengths of competitors' offerings. Before any marketing strategy can be determined or brand positioning strategy implemented it is essential that the market's perceptions are known.

8.5.1 The positioning map

Perceptual mapping is based on a variety of mathematical or qualitative approaches designed to place or describe consumers' or business customers' perceptions of brands or products on one or a series of 'spatial maps'. It is a means of visually depicting customers' perceptions, showing the relative positionings of different brands or products (and thereby companies).

The core attributes must be identified through qualitative research, with follow-up confirmatory research identifying the relative positionings of the brands or companies to be plotted. For example, a perceptual map of the UK furniture market, identified 'value for money' as the key attribute. Research showed that consumers were in reality more concerned with price and specifically product quality than availability, store location, customer service, delivery or aftermarket care.

It is important for all marketers to understand the positioning of their products on such a spatial map, vis-à-vis competitors, particularly

FIGURE 8.4 A perceptual map for the car industry

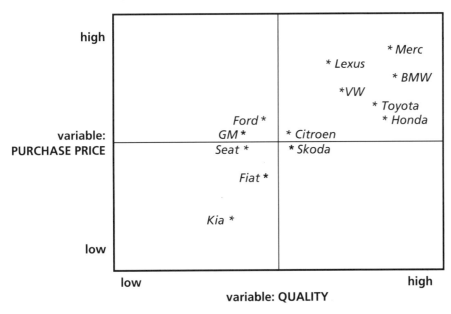

in order to develop realistic and effective marketing programmes. Figure 8.4 presents a completed example for the European car industry. Marketing research identified the variables and the positionings. If more than two variables are thought to be critical, several positioning maps may be constructed. Software exists which plots three or more variables on three-dimensional maps, but in most instances, simple two-dimensional maps as shown in Figure 8.4 are sufficient.

8.5.2 Producing the positioning map in marketing planning

The analyses so far undertaken (see Figures 2.1, 5.3 and 6.2) have ascertained the core Key Customer Values desired or demanded by customers. This work has presented a shopping list or league table of these KCVs. The positioning map should use these leading KCVs as the variables for the X- and Y-axes on one or more perceptual maps. The organization's positionings should be marked on the map or graph along with the positionings for all leading direct and substitute competitors. The relative distances between the companies indicates their ability or inability to satisfactorily match customers' needs for the main KCVs.

FIGURE 8.5 The Positioning map

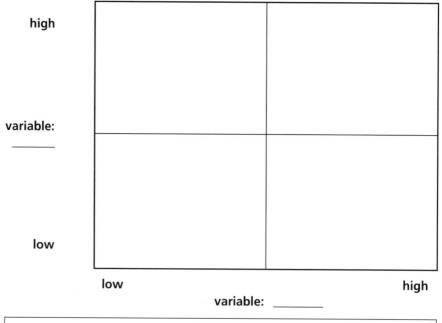

Figure 8.5 presents a blueprint perceptual map, which should now be completed for each target market or market segment. Having established where the organization's products or brands are currently positioned, it is necessary to consider where ideally they should be positioned. This decision should be informed by the marketing analyses, relate to stated priority KCVs and strive to create differentiation against leading competitors. The actions required to achieve any desired shift in positioning must feature in the marketing plan's recommended actions.

SUMMARY

By the end of this chapter the core elements of the marketing strategy should have been determined. These should clearly reflect the organization's mission statement of corporate intent. The market's segments may have been revised; certainly the organization's choice of which segments or customer groupings it wishes to prioritize as targets will have been updated. Within each target market, the company should have evaluated its competitive edge against its rivals to determine any differential advantage or, at worst, the strengths it will be best placed to emphasize in its marketing programmes. Finally, in each priority target market, there should be a clear recommendation for how the organization's products and brands should be positioned against its rivals. This positioning strategy must be implemented and communicated through the marketing plan's recommended marketing programmes, outlined in Chapter 11.

9

Strategy recommendations

The previous chapter outlined the requirements for determining an updated marketing strategy. The organization must have clear and specific recommendations in terms of opportunities to pursue, target markets, its basis for competing and desired brand positioning. The purpose of this chapter is to crystallize these recommendations to ensure there are no ambiguous statements which can be misinterpreted within the marketing function and in the other functional areas of the organization. The resulting marketing programmes at the heart of the marketing plan must relate to this marketing strategy and contain:

- clarification of opportunities and target market priorities;
- agreement of desired brand positionings and bases for competing;
- identification of any barriers to proceeding with the marketing strategy.

9.1 STRATEGIES SHOULD CHANGE

The background analyses (Chapters 2 and 3) have highlighted the strengths and weaknesses implicit in the current view of core target markets, and the need to update key customer targets. The additional analyses (Chapters 4–8) have brought together detailed information relating to the market and its current characteristics: customer needs and expectations; general market trends and impacting aspects of the external marketing environment; competitive positions and competitors' strengths; the basis for competing and differential advantage; brand or product positionings; and strengths, weaknesses, opportunities and threats. In particular, analyses of the marketing environment and SWOT issues have revealed opportunities to consider, and analyses of customers and competitors have also suggested emerging possibilities. The attractiveness criteria of the DPM, the ABC sales: contribution analysis and the product life cycle assessment have provided objective measures for assessing the relative merits of these opportunities vis-à-vis existing operations and activities.

In the light of this information and these analyses, strategy decisions have now been made (Figure 8.2):

- the opportunities to be pursued;
- which groups of customers to target;
- with what positioning or offering;
- on what competitive basis.

9.2 REVISING THE TARGETING STRATEGY

By now, it should be clear that there is a need to revise the selection of key customer targets and of key target markets. These conclusions should be based on much more than a simple understanding of buyer purchasing behaviour and general market trends. Competitors' positions and strategies; the organization's strengths and weaknesses; the basis for competing and any differential advantages; the product life cycle and the need for a balanced portfolio, are all issues which should play a role in determining target market strategy. As shown, the DPM has considerable potential in objectively agreeing priorities and revising target market selection.

Where such detailed marketing analyses have been undertaken, the need for some revisions to an organization's targeting priorities will have been revealed. Marketing plans should reflect these market developments and strategy choices, ensuring the recommended marketing programmes reflect market drivers and strategy decisions.

9.3 THE NEED TO STRIVE FOR A DIFFERENTIAL ADVANTAGE

All organizations strive to attain or develop a differential advantage for their products or services: a feature perceived by target customers to be (a) highly desirable, and (b) not offered by rival companies. Most organizations fail to determine such an advantage, but those which do clearly have an advantage in their markets. As Section 8.4 has outlined, it is essential to seek a differential advantage (DA) or competitive edge for each product or service in each target market. Where a DA is identified, it must be stressed in all associated sales and marketing programmes and in the positioning strategy. At the very worst, a compelling set of strengths must be positioned attractively in order to appeal to targeted customers.

9.4 REQUIRED POSITIONING

Using a positioning perceptual map as an aid (see Figures 8.4 and 8.5), it is necessary to explain, for each target market or segment, the required product or brand positioning vis-à-vis the key competitors along the key customer values (KCVs) identified in Figures 2.1 and 5.3. Remember, these dimensions must be seen as important by the customers rather than by just the organization's own executives.

This is a fundamental step in the determination of the strategy. The stated required positioning must:

- be based on customers' identified needs;
- take into account competitors' positionings and their ability to deliver to these customer needs;
- maximize any identified differential advantage;
- feed into sales and marketing programmes.

One of the principal aims of the eventual marketing programmes, as discussed in Chapter 11, must be to offer products and services which deliver this desired positioning to the targeted customers, with programmes which communicate the proposition to these target customers.

9.5 STRATEGY SUMMARY

In the light of the core analyses so far undertaken, the following questions now need to be answered. What are:

(a) The primary opportunities to pursue? Why these?

(b) The core markets to target? Why these?

(c) The required product positioning strategies? Why these?

(d) The fundamental differential advantages?

(e) The priorities for the organization?

In order to establish clarity within the organization and to correctly steer the marketing programmes recommended in the marketing plan, the key strategic decisions now need to be summarized: see Figure 9.1. Any warning signs or obvious impediments to following the emerging marketing strategy should now be considered in case the proposals are seriously flawed or doomed to failure because of resourcing, operational, leadership or behavioural problems.

FIGURE 9.1   Marketing strategy summary statement

Emerging opportunity to pursue + existing opportunities to support	Principal reasons	Key target markets or market segments

Core targeted segments/markets						
Segment	1:	2:	3:	4:	5:	6:
Principal reason for segment being targeting priority						
Likely sales Current year (units) Likely sales next year						
KCVs per segment						
Required brand positioning						
Main two competitors						
Principal competitive threat						
Differential advantage (DA)						
Key problems to overcome						
Capital implications from strategy						

- **This is the overall statement of marketing strategy and must be fully completed**

SUMMARY

The organization must have clear and specific recommendations in terms of opportunities to pursue, target markets, the basis for competing and desired brand positioning. Implications from these aims in terms of problems and resourcing should be considered. These recommendations must be concisely summarized in order to ensure there are no ambiguous statements which can be misinterpreted within the marketing function and in the other functional areas of the organization. The resulting marketing programmes at the heart of the marketing plan must relate to this marketing strategy and the proposed actions should execute its recommendations.

10

Marketing objectives and gap analysis

The marketing strategy must be operationalized. This requires the formulation of specific objectives and goals. Marketing objectives are an essential part of the marketing plan, giving a sense of direction to the specified marketing programmes. Without such objectives there is no record of what the marketing plan is trying to achieve, when, or whether it has been successful! Gap analysis examines recent variations between forecasts for perhaps sales volumes or profitability and the actual achieved figures, illustrating the nature of the marketing task in hand. It is a useful technique for ensuring over-ambitious goals are tempered and for encouraging lagging colleagues to think ahead with a desire for new ideas and plans. This chapter will help to:

- translate the marketing strategy into achievable milestones;
- specify marketing objectives against which progress may be evaluated;
- explain the role of gap analysis in marketing planning.

10.1 MARKETING OBJECTIVES

Marketing objectives play a critical role in the execution of marketing strategy. These are set in relation to the earlier marketing analysis to be synergistic with the identified market trends and consistent with strengths, weaknesses and the competitive situation. The resulting marketing objectives must be designed to implement the marketing strategy as summarized in Figure 9.1.

It is quite usual for some objectives to be broad while others are quite specific. Figure 10.1 has been designed to cope with these differences by asking first for general objectives and then for a more detailed view that is target market focused. Start with the general strategic objectives, but try to limit these to between six and eight, then move on to the more specific target market objectives. Remember that marketing objectives should be expressed in specific terms and must be capable of measurement. They should cover all options in terms of new and existing products/services as well as new and existing target markets. This means the objectives should address a combination of the following:

- existing products or services in existing markets;
- new products or services for existing markets;
- existing products or services for new markets;
- new products or services for new markets.

These objectives should be described in terms of values, volumes and market shares and should have a clearly defined timescale. These details will help to refine subsequent marketing programmes for implementation, as described in Chapter 11.

Subsequent assessments of performance and evaluations of progress in operationalizing the marketing plan should take account of these stated objectives.

FIGURE 10.1 Marketing objectives

General strategic marketing objectives	
•	
•	
•	
•	
•	
•	
Segment:	Objective:
Segment:	Objective:
Segment:	Objective:
Segment:	Objective:
Segment:	Objective:
Segment:	Objective:
• First list overall marketing strategy objectives • Indicate the most important differences for leading target markets • Include a time scale for each objective	

10.2 GAP ANALYSIS

Gap analysis is a useful tool for helping organizations achieve their strategic goals. The first step is to plot recent and current turnover or volume achievements on the gap analysis graph, such as that in Figure 10.2. This is followed by plotting forecast turnover or volume on the basis of no assumed changes to the current strategy: that is where the company would be if it continued as previously and simply maintained the *status quo*. Expectations must be realistic: there is a danger that marketing plans fail because those preparing them set targets which are not achievable. The space between the two lines – the actual and predicted figures – represents the *gap* which the marketing plan's proposed marketing programmes must fill if the new targets are to be achieved.

In order to fill any gaps, there are four strategic options:

(i) *Market Penetration* (MP) – increased market penetration and productivity through, for example, more sales calls, cost reduction, decreased prices, better product or customer mix, etc.
(ii) *Market Development* or *Extension* (ME) – by finding new markets for existing products.
(iii) *New Product Development* (NPD) – the development of new or improved products for existing markets.

FIGURE 10.2 The gap chart

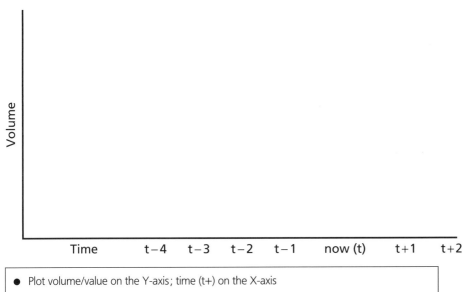

- Plot volume/value on the Y-axis; time (t+) on the X-axis
- Determine the scope of the "gap" and reasons behind it
- What are the options: MP = Market Penetration; ME = Market Extension; NPD = New Product Development; D = Diversification?
- -:-:- = Projected Volume; ——— = desired Volume

(iv) *Diversification* (D) – the development of new products for new markets through, for example, changing the asset base, investment or acquisition.

Consideration must be given to the current product life cycle stage (Section 7.2) and to the competitive positions (Section 6.4), to ensure that recommendations reflect the required product portfolio moves (Section 7.1) and are realistic in terms of competitors' actions and strengths.

As a result of the gap analysis, there should be a better idea of how the *gap* can most effectively be filled. This provides a natural link with the marketing programmes which are developed in the next chapter.

SUMMARY

The gap analysis shows for the recent past how close to forecast financial targets the organization has been. Reasons for significant gaps are examined, in order to make this plan's recommendations more realistic. The marketing plan's marketing objectives must be clear, building from the stated marketing strategy. Otherwise, the organization's actions will not execute the stated marketing strategy or reflect the underlying drivers in the market. The marketing objectives need to determine whether the organization's thrust and required products are focusing on existing markets with current or new products and services, or new markets with current or new products and services. This is not a difficult or time-consuming aspect of marketing planning, but it is a necessary step to ensure the company's sales and marketing activities implement the agreed marketing strategy and reflect the findings from the various marketing analyses.

11

Required marketing programmes

In order to execute the marketing strategy recommendations, it is necessary to consider what marketing programmes are now required. Decisions must be made about which existing activities should be discontinued and how the organization will succeed in the targeted markets. These questions must be addressed and detailed action programmes specified. Such marketing programmes form the core content of a marketing plan. This chapter provides coverage of the essential marketing programme considerations.

If the marketing analyses have identified issues the organization needs to address, then appropriate action needs to be taken in relation to the sales and marketing activities. Without such action, the organization will be ill-equipped for forthcoming encounters with its competitors. These marketing programmes must be specific, engaging, properly costed and capable of implementation – achievable given the resources available. Above all, these programmes must reflect the analyses undertaken and the strategy recommendations made by:

- ensuring the issues from the analyses are tackled;
- scoping product, service, pricing, channel and marketing communication requirements;
- achieving stated marketing objectives.

11.1 ISSUES TO EMPHASIZE

There are some core issues which need to be stressed during the development of the marketing mix programmes: key customer values (KCVs), competitive threats, and any differential advantages over rivals (see Figure 11.1). The marketing programmes must be developed with the intention of satisfying customers, matching or beating competitors'

FIGURE 11.1   Summary by target market of KCVs and DAs

	Target market or segment 1	Target market or segment 2	Target market or segment 3	Target market or segment 4	Target market or segment 5	Target market or segment 6
Summary of KCVs						
Main competitive threat to the company						
Any company DA? Which strengths to leverage?						
Desired product or brand positioning?						

moves, while emphasizing any strengths or differential advantages and achieving the desired brand positioning. They should also reflect market drivers and SWOT concerns.

When formulating marketing programmes, an understanding of current marketing programmes is needed. First, it is necessary to remember what marketing programmes are currently in place. Although many of these existing activities may continue, the revised target market strategy is likely to have implications for the marketing programmes moving forward.

There are five fundamental areas to be addressed: product, pricing, promotion, distribution (channels to market) and people/service – known as the elements of *the marketing mix*.

11.2 THE MARKETING MIX

In order to understand areas of weakness, it is important to flag up current *perceptions* in the target markets for brand awareness; product awareness; product image; quality of deliverable/product; after sales liaison/support and technical expertise; value of deliverable/product; product performance; on-time delivery and service professionalism versus the main competitors. One summary chart is usually sufficient: see Figure 11.2. This emphasizes where improvements are needed. The marketing programmes outlined in the marketing plan must achieve these improvements.

The Marketing Mix is the tool kit of any marketing department, consisting of the '5 Ps': Product (or service), Pricing, Place (distribution/ channels to market), Promotion and People. Each target market requires a bespoke marketing mix or set of marketing programmes.

● *Product* – actions for product additions, modifications, deletions, design, positioning, branding products or services.

- *Price* – pricing/payment policies to be followed for each product group in each target market or segment.
- *Place* – policies for distribution channels and customer service levels.
- *Promotion* – policies for communicating with customers, dealers/distributors and the sales force through advertising, sales promotion, public relations and publicity, exhibitions/trade shows, direct mail, sponsorship, personal selling/the sales force, e-marketing and interactive media.
- *People* – individuals involved in delivering aspects of the service or product – and of the sales and marketing programmes – to customers and those concerned with handling sales and service.

The required *product/service mix* must be specified per target market, particularly if additional products or derivatives are required (Figure 11.3). It is also important to determine the required *Service Levels* necessary to support this product mix (Figures 11.4 and 11.11).

Promotional programmes (marketing communications) are one of the mainstays of marketing activity. The first step is to summarize what promotional work and campaigns have been running recently (do not assume everyone who should know does!). Next, the promotional objectives for any required promotional work need to be stated (e.g. to build brand awareness; re-position a product against competitors; emphasize a particular application, etc.). Finally, suitable promotional programmes (e.g. literature, exhibitions, personal calls, on-line, etc.) and required scheduling should be suggested. Involving a range of personnel with relevant expertise and knowledge in these decisions can be productive. Figures 11.5 to 11.7 provide summary formats. Remember, the promotional programmes must communicate the desired brand positioning to the targeted customers and emphasize any differential advantages over rivals.

Channels to market (distribution): on the proforma provided (Figure 11.8) summarize any changes now required to distribution and channels to targeted customers. If an organization has direct relationships with customers, this aspect is likely to be of little importance. However, there may be sales opportunities from relationships with partners, contractors or consultants, plus from licensing (Figure 11.9). Channels to market are important and links with suppliers or partners can provide sales leads.

For *pricing*, there are many instances where pricing is well known and 'retail' oriented. Against this background there are various questions to address. What pricing policy and price point changes are required? Owing to product or marketing mix differentiation, is there an opportunity for premium pricing? What can be learned from competitors' bids? What are customers' bid requirements? Why are bids lost? Answering these questions enables appropriate fine-tuning or changes in the organization's pricing/bidding policy and procedures to be made for the target markets under review (Figure 11.1). Such decisions must take into consideration the identified desired brand positioning and competitors' positionings.

The following ten summary proformas highlight the principal aspects of the marketing programme recommendations. Each is a necessary component of an effective and robust marketing plan:

11.2   Customer perceptions – the organization versus leading rivals
11.3   Summary of required product/service mix
11.4   Required service levels to support the product mix
11.5   Summary of current advertising and promotion
11.6   Key promotional activity required
11.7   Desired promotional programmes
11.8   Summary of marketing channel requirements
11.9   Sales links through suppliers/contractors/partners
11.10 Summary of pricing policy changes
11.11 Process/customer liaison improvements required

FIGURE 11.2   Customer perceptions – the organization versus leading rivals

	Current perceptions – segment: _____				
	Positive		**Neutral**	**Negative**	
	++	**+**	**+/–**	**–**	**– –**
Brand awareness					
Product awareness					
Product/brand image					
Quality of product/ deliverable					
After sales liaison/support					
Value of product/ deliverable					
Product performance					
On-time delivery					
Service professionalism					
Technical expertise					
Other:					
Other:					
Other:					

NB: Competitor 1 is: Competitor 2 is:

- Produce one proforma per targeted segment
- First enter the organization's own rating: ++, +, +/–, – or – –. NB: ++ = very positive/good; +/– = neutral; – – = highly negative/very poor
- Second enter the ratings for the two leading rivals in the segment
- Use this coding to mark companies on the chart: 0 = the organization; 1 = main rival; 2 = second main rival. Name these competitors on the proforma

In the context of these perceptions and the standing versus leading rivals, on which features must the organization immediately focus?

FIGURE 11.3 Summary of required product/service mix

Target market or segment	Title of the organization's relevant product or service	Product or service description
1		
2		
3		
4		

- List out existing products/services pertinent to each target market's or segment's needs and KCVs
- Column 2 = popular name/acronym; column 3 = "lay person's" description

Segment/market	Additional product/ service requirements	Product/service attributes	Why required

- In this section, detail any new/additional products needed in the light of the marketing analyses to maintain the organization's competitive position, facilitate the organization's target market strategy or address identified opportunities
- Note, the "new product" could be a hybrid of activities which cuts across the organization's divisions/departments/sectors

FIGURE 11.4 Required service levels to support the product mix

	Segment 1	Segment 2	Segment 3	Segment 4
People				
Advice/guidance				
Ongoing support				
Facilities				
Other:				
Other:				
Training requirements				
Resource implications				

- This Figure requests information concerning service aspects of the product offer. The products *per se* (their tangible attributes) are detailed in Figure 11.3
- Some service aspects will require retraining/orientation of personnel interfacing with customers
- These "soft" issues connected with the product offering – such as warranties, technical advice, consumer finance, parts availability, etc – will require resourcing

FIGURE 11.5   Summary of current advertising and promotion

Nature of campaign
What was done, when, which promotional mix elements

Campaign objectives
For example, create brand awareness; generate sales leads; counteract rival's
    campaign; support new product launch; etc

Cost of programme (if known)

Results of programme (if known)

- Complete a proforma per targeted segment
- Note: the promotional mix includes advertising, publicity and public relations, sales
    promotion, personal selling, sponsorship, direct mail and literature, as well as the internet
    and direct communications – all forms of promotional activity

FIGURE 11.6 Key promotional activity required

Promotional task	\multicolumn{8}{c}{Targeted markets or segments}
	1	**2**	**3**	**4**	**5**	**6**	**7**	**8**
Build brand awareness								
Build brand image								
Build product awareness								
Build product image								
Position against competitors								
Re-position against competitors								
Create primary demand for product								
Induce trial								
Influence customers' KCVs								
Generate sales leads								
Promote after sales liaison								
Influence customer buying process								
Nurture ongoing relationship								
Promote collaboration								
Promote within the organization								
Other:								
Other:								
Other:								

- Indicate promotional requirements per targeted segment
- Keep selections to the bare minimum – too many will not be feasible or cost effective. If most boxes are ticked, revisit the list to prioritize

FIGURE 11.7   Desired promotional programmes

Promotion objectives (priorities)
Suggested advertising and promotions programmes Including likely tools/techniques
Anticipated budget required
Timing and scheduling of promotional activity
Agency/supplier
● Complete a proforma per targeted segment/market

FIGURE 11.8 Summary of marketing channel requirements

NB: If no dealers/distributors are involved in sales transactions, ignore this proforma!

Target market/segment: _____ Requirement:
Target market/segment: _____ Requirement:
Target market/segment: _____ Requirement:
Target market/segment: _____ Requirement:
Overall policy changes:
Personnel and service improvements required:
● State required dealer and distribution changes necessary to facilitate the target market strategy and associated marketing programmes (a) per core segment, (b) overall in the territory/market

FIGURE 11.9 Sales links through suppliers/contractors/partners

NB: This is relevant to organizations enjoying direct relationships with customers

Market/segment:_____
Nature of links with suppliers/contractors/consortium partners
Scope for the organization to use links for sales leads
Requirements to enable the organization to use these links
● Existing links/working relationships with third parties or intermediaries such as suppliers, contractors, consortium partners may form the basis for generating sales leads if handled with such an aim

FIGURE 11.10   Summary of pricing policy changes

Target market or market segment	The organization				Principal competitor:_____			
	Achieved price (A)	Desired price or bid price (D)	A–D(+/–) and reason for discrepancy	Product name		Achieved price (A)	Desired price (D)	A–D (+/–)

Summary of required pricing changes and pricing/bid policy alterations

- Inevitably the analyses will have revealed the need to modify pricing. The stated strategy will also require changes to pricing policies
- If information is known about the leading competitor, include it. Identify this competitor
- If bid problems are relevant and known/realized, explain in the lower section of box

In the light of the marketing analyses, are there any pricing policy changes required?

Of current pricing/bid arrangements, what aspects are worthy of development? What features are causing problems?

FIGURE 11.11   Process/customer liaison improvements required

Area requiring attention	Explanation/definition	Required action
Market information		
Product information		
Flows of information for bids/pricing		
Demonstrations		
Handling enquiries		
Pre-delivery advice		
Commercial support to customers		
Technical support		
Back-up advice		
Payment conditions/customer credit		
Inter-personnel relationships		
Communication with clients		
Handling visits		
Communication with suppliers		
Feedback to clients/suppliers		
Training		
Other:		
Other:		

- This is the organization helping customers; making life easier for customers to deal with the organization; improving flows of information and communications

SUMMARY

The core output from any marketing planning exercise must be detailed action plans which outline the marketing mix programmes for each targeted market. It is essential that these programmes aim to satisfy customers' needs, relate to the identified key customer values (KCVs), take account of market trends and the organization's competitive position, while fully utilizing any differential advantage held over rivals and seeking to achieve the desired brand positioning.

This chapter has presented summary proformas for all of the core elements of well constructed marketing programmes: product (or service) requirements, pricing and payment issues, marketing channel selection and distribution control, promotional activity and personnel/customer service needs. Until each of these marketing programme components has been examined and specific recommendations made, there is no marketing plan and the determined marketing strategy will not be implemented. The recommended programme must closely relate to the stated marketing objectives in the previous chapter.

12

Resources, schedules and responsibilities

Many marketing plans produce detailed marketing mix action lists without following through to determine the full costs of these programmes and whether all activities are viable. Such poorly specified plans often fail to state when the programmes need to run or consider whether there are scale economies for certain activities across product groups or market segments. All too often the tasks are not allocated to specific departments or managers, with the result that many well-founded recommendations simply do not happen. This short chapter with three summary charts helps to focus those involved in marketing planning to consider these key considerations: budgets, timing and the allocation of responsibilities, for example in the following areas:

- rolling out the marketing plan's recommendations;
- presenting personnel with clear direction;
- ensuring budgets, schedules and responsibilities are specified.

12.1 RESOURCES, SCHEDULING AND RESPONSIBILITIES

Many of the marketing planning recommendations will only lead to a few changes in current activity and spending. However, some aspects of the proposed marketing programmes will be new. A summary of programme tasks is needed so that specific managers are made responsible for their implementation and become accountable for owning *particular* aspects of the marketing plan. Clear guidelines for the timing (scheduling) of the programme tasks must be made to avoid clashes between product groups or across segments, to aid internal communications and to ensure the core marketing requirements do actually take place. If

FIGURE 12.1   Summary of programme tasks, timing and costs

Programme or marketing mix task	Person or department responsible	Date(s) for activity	Anticipated cost	Implications for the organization

- The main marketing mix requirements from Chapter 11 should be entered in column 1
- People must now take "ownership" of the identified actions in Chapter 11 and determine schedules and programme costs

costs are to be kept under control, managers must not be allowed to produce extensive 'wish lists' of activities. A realistic check on the achievable marketing activities must be maintained. Figure 12.1 presents a summary of these important issues. Completion of this summary forces colleagues to take 'ownership' of the required actions.

It may be necessary to consolidate these details into summary statements of responsibilities by name/department, by month, and under convenient budget headings (Figures 12.2 and 12.3). There may well be external suppliers/agencies contracted to deliver specific actions, particularly in terms of promotional requirements and their actions/deliverables must be captured.

Senior managers will seek reassurance that rewards will outweigh costs, which anyway they will want to ensure have been kept to a minimum. A poorly costed marketing plan is unlikely to be signed off by the organization's leadership team or deliver improvements in performance for the company.

F I G U R E   1 2 . 2   Summary of responsibilities

Person or department	Responsibility/task	Dates/timings	External supplier/ agency

- Allocate the tasks detailed in Figure 12.1 to individual managers or departments
- Specify when these activities must take place

F I G U R E   1 2 . 3   Summary of costs and budget implications

Task	Cost	Any budget implications for the organization?

- Summarize the costs/budgets for each of the marketing programme activities detailed in Chapter 11
- Outline any implications from the combined totals of these costs

SUMMARY

This chapter has brought to the marketing planning process an important set of operational and implementation considerations. For the marketing plan to be actioned and the detailed marketing mix recommendations implemented, personnel must take on the responsibility of ensuring the recommended tasks take place, that clear schedules are produced and that full costings are determined with an assessment of the overall budgetary implications and probable rewards for the organization.

13

Additional implications, ongoing needs and monitoring the marketing plan's effectiveness

The detailed strategy and implementation recommendations made within the marketing plan will have implications for other departments outside marketing. Product designers, production personnel, sales and distribution managers, BD executives, HR and treasury departments as well as senior management will need to (a) understand the direction of the plan, (b) believe in its rationale and rigour of analysis, (c) agree to change some of their practices and activities, and (d) be fully briefed in order to fulfil their contributions to the plan. Some canvassing or lobbying by those producing the marketing plan will be necessary.

No matter how much work goes in to marketing planning, the analyses are never fully complete and there will always be information gaps. The mechanisms for filling these gaps will need to be agreed. This may involve specifying an ongoing programme of marketing research. The marketing mix requirements cannot all be actioned immediately: new product development takes time, customer service modifications require training and controls, distribution improvements may require lengthy negotiations and contractual changes with third parties. These issues must be highlighted.

Decisions about how the marketing plan will be monitored must be made. This involves judging how recommendations have been carried out and considering the most appropriate measures of the plan's effectiveness. The benchmarks against which such judgements will be made must be agreed. This chapter will consider:

- the implications from the marketing plan's recommendations on other departments within the organization;
- ongoing work and marketing research needs;
- the monitoring of the marketing plan's implementation and progress.

13.1 ADDITIONAL IMPLICATIONS ACROSS THE ORGANIZATION

The marketing strategy and target market selection recommendations and supporting marketing programmes will have ramifications for other functions within the business: R&D, sales, BD, finance, partnerships, channels to market, facilities, production are all are among those areas likely to be affected. The likely scale and scope of such effects now need to be considered (Figure 13.1). The outputs must be conveyed to the company's leadership team and affected line managers, so that someone can be charged with monitoring and controlling these issues.

FIGURE 13.1   Summary of anticipated knock-on impacts

Area of impact	Implication/required action/by whom

- Detail the likely knock-on impacts
- Consider the action required to facilitate the plan's unhindered implementation

13.2 ONGOING NEEDS

The analyses will have identified weaknesses in the organization's marketing information. A priority is considering the most pressing outstanding information gaps and how best to gather such marketing intelligence (Figure 13.2). In addition, there will be aspects of the

FIGURE 13.2 Ongoing marketing research requirements

Information gap	Likely research activity	Timing	Cost
● Specify required marketing research activity			

FIGURE 13.3 Medium-term work required

Area	Required work
Internal structuring/operations	
Market development	
Resource base	
Products and product mix	
Sales force and customer service	
Marketing channels	
Promotional activity/evaluation	
Pricing and payment terms	
Training	
Recruitment	
Other:	
● Specify the longer term marketing requirements	

marketing strategy and marketing mix requirements which cannot be addressed immediately. These areas should be pinpointed for future attention so that key aspects of the marketing plan's recommendations are not lost (Figure 13.3).

13.3 MONITORING EFFECTIVENESS AND PROGRESS

Monitoring progress is a crucial element of any marketing planning programme. The extent to which the marketing strategy and marketing objectives in the marketing plan have been executed must be gauged and a judgement made about whether these have resulted in the expected gains for the organization.

FIGURE 13.4 Monitoring the performance

Monitored issue	Expected result (6 mths)	Actual outcome (6 mths)	Reason for gap	Expected result (12 mths)	Actual outcome (12 mths)	Reason for gap

- Determine measures for benchmarking progress
- Expected results should include sales, contributions, attitudinal data relating to customers' perceptions of brand positioning and their views on customer satisfaction

The final stage of any marketing planning exercise is to ensure that procedures are set up for monitoring the effectiveness of the plan. There are two parts to this important stage of the process. First, periodically review whether the stated marketing objectives (Chapter 10) have been achieved. Make a note of when the reviews will take place, what form they should follow and who will be involved. Formalizing this part of the monitoring process will help to ensure that the review really happens. It is also important to check that the marketing planning process is improving the financial health and status of the organization.

The second part of the monitoring process involves systematically updating the marketing analyses as more information becomes available. Customer needs, competitors' strategies, market trends, SWOTs, bases for competing and brand positionings will all be subject to change over time. By incorporating new information into the analyses, a useful impression is gained of the more subtle changes brought about by the marketing plan. The updating additionally gives a head start for developing the next period's plan.

It may be useful to complete Figure 13.4 to identify the organization's performance in relation to the objectives set and other areas considered to be important. The monitored issues column has been left blank enabling a choice of which areas to revisit.

There will be criteria relating to the stated marketing objectives (Chapter 10) in the marketing plan and the specified marketing actions to include in Figure 13.4. There are other issues to consider concerning performance, as discussed in the next chapter.

SUMMARY

The marketing plan will have raised issues which affect other areas of the organization outside the marketing function. These knock-on implications need to be fully considered. Appropriate canvassing of colleagues will also be required to aid the unhindered implementation of the plan's recommendations.

In addition, the chapter has considered the marketing research and ongoing marketing programme developments which cannot be immediately addressed but which must be tackled in the medium term if momentum is to be maintained. Finally, the marketing plan's implementation and effectiveness must be monitored against wide ranging and carefully thought out benchmarks, including a balanced scorecard so that not only financial measures are utilized.

14

Controlling implementation of the marketing plan

An essential aspect of effective marketing planning is to establish adequate performance measures. Related to this core foundation for success is the need to formally review progress and take appropriate remedial action. This section of *Marketing Planning* briefly outlines possible performance metrics to adopt before presenting an auditing template designed to assist in controlling the roll-out of the marketing plan. There must be adequate controls to ensure the implementation of a marketing plan and to help address the inevitable obstacles impeding its roll-out. Part Four provides additional guidance for launching and controlling a marketing planning programme within an organization and managing the resulting marketing plan. This chapter deals with:

- creating performance standards;
- marketing controls;
- reviews and audits.

14.1 ESTABLISHING PERFORMANCE STANDARDS

Planning and controlling are closely linked because plans include statements about what is to be achieved. These statements function as performance standards and establish the expectations of the organization's leadership team. A performance standard is an expected level of performance against which actual performance can be compared. Performance standards might be in terms of sales targets, customer satisfaction measures, levels of brand awareness, new business wins, profitability, improved customer retention, improvements in product quality or productivity gains. They will be unique to each organization, its values and current market position. However, best practice suggests that a balanced set of criteria should be adopted. All organizations include financial measures of performance, which are necessary in order to satisfy stakeholders and shareholders. Measuring the success of marketing planning, however, often involves using some of the 'softer' issues listed in Table 14.1, right-hand column, below.

TABLE 14.1   Popular performance standards

Key marketing financial performance standards	Leading non-financial marketing performance standards
Revenue growth	Customer satisfaction
Return on investment	Delivery performance
Product profitability	New customers gained
Customer profitability	Market share
Return on sales	Customer loyalty
Total return to shareholders	Customer dissatisfaction
Return on capital employed	Brand awareness
Sales per square metre (for retailers)	Lost customers
	Price level achieved
	Customer brand attitudes

14.2 MARKETING CONTROLS

To compare actual performance with performance standards, marketing managers should know what marketers within the company are doing and must have information about the activities of any external organizations providing marketing assistance. Actual performance is compared with expectations or targets for the agreed performance standards. Any discrepancies must be diagnosed and appropriate action taken to rectify the situation.

There are many reasons for poor performance. The targets may be unrealistic, personnel may not have bought-in to the plan or may be unclear about their role in operationalizing it, other strategic priorities may be blocking progress, resources and capabilities may be inadequate or poorly timed, required skills and expertise may be lacking, organizational restructuring or changing personnel may have impeded the roll-out of the plan, or unexpected market dynamics may be limiting progress. These are just some of the possible problems. Diagnosing these problems and scoping out the challenges faced is critical if corrective action is to be prescribed. If senior managers fail to look for problems in the implementation of the marketing plan, roll-out is unlikely to be effective. The operationalization of plans is never trouble-free. By accepting that difficulties are likely, problems can quickly be revealed and appropriate remedies put in place.

14.3 REVIEWS AND AUDITS

Once the marketing plan has been developed, it must be implemented. Ensuring that specific actions have been allocated to individual managers is part of the solution. Clearly defined timeframes, budgets and performance measures must be agreed for these actions. The management of implementation also requires the monitoring of progress against agreed performance expectations. Review sessions and adopting a 'name and shame' approach can be helpful in achieving these expectations.

Review meetings

Review sessions are an integral part of the marketing planning process. These generally take one of two forms: (a) business unit teams present to senior managers and explain their progress in rolling-out their part of the company's marketing plan; (b) cross-functional workshops which enable progress to be fully reviewed, exploring emerging issues and determining appropriate remedial actions. A typical agenda for such a session is:

1 Review the current strategy. Focus on the plan's product/service propositions and how effectively they are being taken to the specified target market segments.

2 Examine what is working and what is not! This involves learning about successes in the process and emulating them. The identification of problems to fix is of fundamental importance.

3 Determine appropriate actions. Specify tasks and responsibilities as a result of the discussion.

Generally, such a discussion revolves around:

- product/service propositions to take to market and any required fine-tuning;
- message clarity of the propositions and their communication to target markets;
- marketing communications campaign development and execution;
- communication across the company of the plan and its imperatives;
- orientation of channel partners/members to the revised direction of the plan;
- specialist skills required to help roll out the plan;
- strategy for establishing/managing channel and customer relationships;

- controls and incentives required to change colleagues' behaviours in order to enact the new look marketing strategy and marketing plan;
- establishing appropriate reporting criteria and processes aligned to the plan.

Marketing plans often alter a company's thinking and direction, so a programme of change management is required in order to realign managers, budgets, the sales force and so forth. Detailed planning of how best to align an organization's resources around a marketing plan leads to more successful implementation.

The progress audit

The *progress audit* is used as an input to the review meeting or as a standalone activity. This is a comprehensive examination of trends in a market linked to the assessment of performance. Reasons for underperformance are revealed in this process. The *progress audit* has been developed to assist in controlling the roll-out of a marketing plan, identifying quickly where altered decisions and actions may be required.

The Dibb/Simkin *progress audit* includes the components shown in Figure 14.1.

FIGURE 14.1   The marketing planning progress audit

Progress in addressing market challenges			
Key identified threats	*Agreed actions in the plan*	*Progress status*	*Remedial recommendations*
Key identified opportunities	*Agreed actions in the plan*	*Progress status*	*Remedial recommendations*
Essential weaknesses to fix	*Agreed actions in the plan*	*Progress status*	*Remedial recommendations*

▶

Progress in marketing strategy roll-out			
Target market strategy priorities	Agreed actions in the plan	Progress status	Remedial recommendations
Segment selection Key account list			
Brand positioning			
Basis for competing			
Product/service mix			
Customer engagement/handling			
MarComms			
Pricing			
Channel issues			
Partner/supplier issues			

Progress in marketing programme roll-out				
Agreed action	Whose task	Scheduled date	Current status of action	Recommendation

Performance assessment			
Stated performance expectation	Current performance	Nature of any gap	Recommendations

Addressing under-performance		
Under-performance issues	*Reasons identified*	*Recommendations*
Operations		
Marketing		
Delivery to the customer		
Others		

Capability and resource deficiencies to fix	
Gaps and deficiencies in capabilities	*Recommendations*
Resourcing problems	*Recommendations*

Market dynamics and emerging challenges	
Key challenges in the market	*Recommendations*
Competitor reaction/activities	
Customer response/requirements	
Marketing environment forces	
Supply chain issues	

SUMMARY

Assessing the effectiveness of the marketing plan and the identification of blockers to performance relies on establishing appropriate performance metrics. The agreed set of performance measures should include 'softer' marketing considerations alongside necessary financial measures of performance. It is essential that the annual marketing planning season is not the only time when performance is judged.

Regular review meetings should be staged in order to identify and reward successes, shame those failing to deliver, reveal problems, agree remedial actions and to maintain momentum behind the roll-out of the marketing plan. The *progress audit* is a useful way for formalizing the ongoing assessment of progress, ensuring appropriate remedial actions are specified, allocated to named managers and followed through.

Part Three overviews the structure of a marketing plan. Part Four of *Marketing Planning* explores in more detail how best to instigate a marketing planning programme and to manage the implementation of the resulting marketing plan.

THE MARKETING PLAN

Part Three outlines the nature of the output of the marketing planning process, the marketing plan. Although each organization has its own requirements, there are some essential components to include in an effective and directional marketing plan.

- The scope of the marketing plan.

- The essential components of a robust marketing plan document.

- A blueprint for a well-rounded marketing plan.

15

The marketing plan document

There is no single approved template for an optimum marketing plan. Each organization has its own house style and requirements. The core deliverables of the marketing plan document are the intended marketing programmes and the work plans required to facilitate successful implementation. The marketing plan is a call to action – the articulation of what now must be done by the company in its target markets, when, how, by whom, for what returns and at what costs. While there is no universally agreed structure for an ideal marketing plan, there are various core components to a robust and convincing plan. This Part of *Marketing Planning* examines the essential sections of a well-rounded marketing plan document, by:

- considering the intended scope of the marketing plan;
- exploring the essential components of a robust marketing plan document;
- suggesting a blueprint for a well-rounded marketing plan.

15.1 THE SCOPE OF THE MARKETING PLAN

A core output of marketing planning is the marketing plan. This is a document or blueprint resulting from the marketing planning process examined in Part Two. The marketing planning process involves analysing the marketplace, modifying or updating the recommended marketing strategy accordingly and developing detailed marketing programmes designed to implement the specified marketing strategy. The resulting plan details the required marketing programmes, establishes their costs, nominates review dates and performance metrics, allocates resources, creates a schedule for the programme activities and assigns personnel to these tasks.

The duration of scope for a marketing plan varies in different organizations. Plans that cover a period of one year or less are called short-range plans. Medium-range plans are usually for two to five years. Marketing plans extending beyond five years are generally viewed as long-range plans and are rare. Marketing managers may have short-, medium- and long-range plans all at the same time. As the marketing environment continues to change and business decisions become more complex, profitability and survival will depend more and more on the development of long range plans. However, detailed twelve-month plans are a necessity.

Most organizations annually update their marketing plans, focusing in detail on the imminent twelve months and providing an overview of intentions for the subsequent two years. This provides the organization with a marketing plan covering three years. Modifications in a company's marketing strategy will always be needed to respond to changes in customer needs, the marketing environment and competitors' activities. Assuming the essential marketing analyses are updated, each year's marketing plan is unlikely to be only a repetition of the previous year's plan.

The marketing plan is the written document or blueprint governing all of an organization's marketing activities, including the implementation and control of those activities. As explored in Part One, a marketing plan serves a number of purposes:

- updates the organization's marketing strategy and determines marketing objectives;
- offers a 'road map' for implementing the strategy and achieving its objectives;
- assists in management control and monitoring of implementation of a strategy;
- informs new participants in the plan of their role and function;
- specifies how resources are to be allocated and prioritized;
- stimulates thinking and makes better use of resources;
- assigns responsibilities, tasks and timing;
- makes participants aware of problems, opportunities and threats to address;
- assists in ensuring that an organization is customer-focused, aware of market and competitive movements, realistic in its expectations and prudent in its use of resources;
- aligns the company's leadership team to market conditions and agreed priorities.

These purposes have implications for the content of the resulting marketing plan.

Many companies have separate marketing managers or teams addressing different business sectors, product groups, brands or market segments. Each team typically develops its own marketing plan as appropriate to its marketplace. In such instances, the Marketing or BD Director produces an over-arching and all-inclusive marketing plan summarizing the key aspects of each team's plan. Plans may be written for strategic business units, product lines, individual products or brands, or specific market territories, sectors or market segments.

15.2 KEY SECTIONS OF THE MARKETING PLAN

Although each organization has its own remit and preferred house style, most plans share some common ground. Typically, marketing plans include: an executive summary; a statement of objectives; a brief background to the market and products in question; a summary of the market analysis and an examination of realistic marketing opportunities (a description of environmental forces, competitor activity, customers' needs, market segments and internal capabilities); an outline of marketing strategy, target market priorities, the basis for competing, brand and product positioning; a statement of expected sales patterns; the detail of marketing programmes required to implement the marketing plan and controls; financial requirements and budgets; and any operational considerations that arise from the new marketing plan. The bulk of the document should address the proposed marketing activities in the company's target markets. The following pages consider the major parts of a typical marketing plan, as well as the purpose that each part serves.

Management or executive summary

The *management summary* or *executive summary* (often only one or two pages) should be a concise overview of the entire report, including key aims, overall strategies, fundamental conclusions and salient points regarding the suggested marketing programmes and roll-out requirements. Not many people read an entire report, tending to 'dip in' here and there, so the management summary should be comprehensive and clear. Senior executives, in particular, look for brief summaries of the plan's key points and recommendations.

Marketing objectives

Marketing objectives are for the benefit of senior executives and also the managers tasked with actioning the plan's programmes, to give perspective to the plan and scope out the challenges. Aims and objectives should be stated briefly, but should include reference to the organization's mission statement and corporate goals, objectives and any

FIGURE 15.1 Typical marketing plan content and page allocation

---

Management or executive summary (1–2 pages)

Objectives (1)

Organisation's mission statement
Organisation's objectives
Business unit goals

Product/market background (2–3)

Product range
Market overview
Sales summary

Key marketing analysis (12–15)

Marketing environment trends and market drivers
SWOT implications
Customer issues
Competitors' pressures

Marketing strategies (3–5)
Year one detail + years 2 and 3 headlines:

Priority opportunities to pursue
Core target markets
Basis for competing
Desired positioning

Statement of expected results/forecasts (1–2)
Marketing programmes (12–15)
Year one detail + years 2 and 3 headlines:

Marketing mix requirements
Tasks, responsibilities, schedules

Controls and evaluations (1–2)

Financial implications/budgets (1–2)

Operational implications (1–2)

Appendices (20+)

Research findings
Competitor insights
SWOT details
Performance analysis
Programme content + costs

---

fundamental desires for core product groups or brands. It is important that there is harmony between the organization's corporate strategy and its marketing plan recommendations. This section describes the objectives underlying the marketing plan.

A marketing objective is a statement of what is to be accomplished through marketing activities. It specifies the results expected from marketing efforts. All marketing personnel and those managers involved in operationalizing the marketing plan should understand exactly what they are trying to achieve. The marketing objective should be written in such a way that its accomplishment can be measured accurately. A marketing objective should also indicate the timeframe for accomplishing the objective.

Product/market background

Product/market background is a necessity because not everyone reading the plan will be fully familiar with the products and their markets. Senior managers may be unfamiliar with specific aspects of the product or market, or be out of touch with realities in the market. This section of the marketing plan 'sets the scene', helping the readers (such as a chief executive or advertising manager) to understand the marketing plan.

Marketing analysis

As explored in Part Two, the *analysis* section is the foundation of the marketing planning process. If incomplete or too subjective, the resulting recommendations are likely to be based on an inaccurate view of the market and the company's potential. This section of the plan provides a sound foundation to the recommendations and marketing programmes. It includes analyses of the marketing environment, market trends, customers, competitors, competitive positions and competitors' strategies, the suitability of the company's product or service portfolio and the financial performance of products, market segments and even certain customers. As this lengthy list of subjects implies, effective marketing planning is about much more than just being customer-focused. Marketers need to be careful to include all of these areas in their analyses.

The marketing environment section of the marketing plan describes the current state of the marketing environment, including the legal, political, regulatory, technological, societal/green, economic and competitive forces, as well as ethical considerations. It also makes predictions about future directions of those forces. Environmental forces can hamper an organization in achieving its objectives. Most marketing plans include extensive analyses of competitive, technological, legal and regulatory forces, perhaps even creating separate sections for these influential forces of the marketing environment. It is important to note here that because the forces of the marketing environment are dynamic, marketing plans should be reviewed and modified periodically to adjust to change. This analysis will reveal threats and opportunities, and occasionally strategic windows vis-à-vis competitors.

Marketing exists to enable an organization to meet customers' needs properly. This is particularly true in the marketing planning process. The views, needs and expectations of current and potential customers are important as a basis for formal marketing planning. Without such an understanding and analysis of likely changes in customer requirements, it is impossible to safely target those markets of most benefit to the organization's fortunes. It is also impossible to correctly specify marketing programmes.

Meaningful marketing plans and implementation programmes require a comprehensive analysis of an organization's competitive position in its markets and territories, together with an understanding of rival organization's marketing strategies. Failure to understand or anticipate competitors' likely actions is a major weakness in most organizations. Marketing planning presents an opportunity to rectify this deficiency.

The *SWOT analysis* is an important foundation for most marketing plans, helping to produce realistic and meaningful recommendations. This section in the main body of the report should be kept to a concise overview, with detailed market-by-market or country-by-country SWOTs (and associated explanations) kept to the appendices. The first half of this analysis (strengths and weaknesses) examines the company's position or that of its products, vis-à-vis customers, competitor activity, environmental trends and company resources. The second half of the SWOT takes this review further to examine the opportunities and threats identified and to make recommendations that feed into marketing strategy and the marketing mix. The marketing environment analysis often reveals potential opportunities and threats to include in the SWOT analysis. A potential threat can sometimes be transformed into an opportunity if the analysis is undertaken and if appropriate action is taken.

The result of the SWOT analysis should be a thorough understanding of the organization's status and its standing in its markets. A SWOT analysis must be objective, with evidence provided to support the points cited. The focus should be on issues likely to concern customers. As explained in Part Two, which offers illustrative SWOT analyses, the checklist-style SWOT analysis is popular amongst marketers, particularly as part of a marketing plan.

Marketing strategies

Marketing strategies should emerge clearly where the analyses have been objective and thorough. These will include the opportunities to pursue, the target markets most beneficial to the company, the basis for competing or competitive edge in these markets, and the desired product or brand positioning. The strategy overview part of the marketing plan must be realistic and detailed enough to act upon. The strategy section must also convince the organization's leadership team to support the plan.

Marketing strategy focuses on identifying opportunities to be pursued, defining a target market and developing a marketing mix to gain competitive and customer advantages. There is a degree of overlap between corporate strategy and marketing strategy. Marketing strategy is unique in its responsibility to assess buyer needs and the company's potential for gaining competitive advantage, both of which ultimately must guide the corporate mission. In other words, marketing strategy guides the company's direction in terms of market drivers, customers and competitors. A marketing strategy must be consistent with consumer needs, perceptions and beliefs. Thus this section should describe the company's intended target market strategy and how marketing programmes will be used to develop a product or brand positioning that will satisfy the needs of consumers or business customers in the target markets.

Expected results

Having highlighted in the marketing plan the strategic direction and intention, it is important to explain the *expected results* and financials/sales volumes, so as to show why the strategies should be followed. These forecasts should be quantified, typically as expected units of sales and possible market shares. This stage is important if the required marketing programme budgets are to be approved by senior managers.

Marketing programmes for implementation

Recommendations for *marketing programmes* are the culmination of the various analyses and statements of strategies: exactly what needs to be done, how, when, why and by whom. This section is the focus of the marketing plan, explaining the proposed marketing programmes deemed necessary to achieve the stated goals and to implement the desired strategies. Each market segment to be targeted may require its own, tailor-made marketing programme.

In poor marketing plans, there is a lack of analysis and strategy, with the focus falling immediately on the proposed marketing programme recommendations. Robust planning requires the recommendation of detailed marketing programmes, but only after time has been taken to thoroughly address the core marketing analyses and determine a well-defined marketing strategy.

This section of the marketing plan is of paramount importance, providing the specific details of the marketing activity required to implement the marketing plan and to achieve the organization's strategic goals. Each element of the marketing mix should be discussed in turn, with specific recommendations explained in sufficient detail to enable managers to put them into action. Product, people/service, pricing, channel (distribution) and marketing communications must all be addressed. Tasks should be allocated to personnel and responsibilities clearly identified for actioning these tasks and when. This is the core output of marketing planning: the detailed plan of action for the organization's marketing programmes.

Controls and evaluations

It is essential that *controls and evaluations* are established, along with measures to assess the ongoing implementation of the marketing plan. This section of the plan details how the results of the plan will be measured and when. For example, the results of an advertising campaign designed to increase market share may be measured initially in terms of increases in sales volume or improved brand recognition and acceptance by consumers.

A schedule for comparing the results achieved with the objectives set forth in the marketing plan should be developed. There should be guidelines included outlining who is responsible for monitoring the programme and for taking remedial action if expectations are not being met. As explored in Part Four, failure to review the progress of implementation or to take appropriate remedial actions if expectations are not being met, are common causes for the failure of marketing planning to demonstrate added value within an organization.

Financial measures such as sales volumes, profitability, RoI and market shares typically are included. However, 'softer' issues such as brand awareness and customer satisfaction should also be monitored. Best practice dictates a balanced scorecard of financial and 'softer' customer-facing performance measures be adopted.

Financial implications/required budgets

The proposed marketing programmes should be fully costed, so that the anticipated benefits from implementing the plan's recommendations can be assessed. The *financial implications and required budgets* section outlines the returns expected to the company from implementation of the plan versus the costs associated with implementing the plan's recommendations. The organization's leadership team inevitably will seek reassurance from the plan that projected costs are more than covered by anticipated growth in revenues. The costs incurred will be weighed against expected revenues.

A budget must be prepared in order to allocate resources, so as to accomplish the stated marketing objectives. It should contain estimates of the costs of implementing the plan, including the costs of advertising, sales force training and remuneration, development of distribution channels and marketing research, amongst other tasks. All of the core costs associated with operationalizing the suggested marketing programme should be stated, including staff and other overheads.

Operational considerations

The desired marketing strategy and proposed marketing programmes may have ramifications for other operations in the organization: product groups, brand teams, sectors or territories; for research and development; capital investment decisions; staffing; engineering or production; logistics and supply chain; customer relations; media suppliers and channel management. The *operational implications* must be highlighted and any negative knock-on ramifications brought to the attention of relevant managers. Too much detail may be inappropriate and politically sensitive within the organization, but 'nasty surprises' resulting from the implementation of the plan must be avoided.

Appendices

The main body of the marketing plan should be as concise as possible. However, the document must tell the full story in order to be convincing. It should include evidence and statistics supporting the strategies and marketing programmes being recommended. The ability to effectively implement the plan's recommendations requires that adequate detail be included. In order to balance the need to include evidence, statistics, market data and details of the proposed marketing programmes against the requirement for a concise document that is not off-putting to members of the leadership team, use should be made of *appendices*. These help to keep the report concise and well focused. It is necessary to make sure any included appendices are fully cross-referenced in the main body of the report.

SUMMARY

There is no universally accepted marketing plan template. However, there are 'must include' sections. The scope of the marketing plan may be short-, medium- or long-term. More often than not, there is a three-year focus, with detailed marketing programmes for year one and outline programmes recommended for years two and three.

Many companies have separate marketing managers or teams addressing different business sectors; products, product groups or brands; or territories, market sectors and market segments. Each team typically develops its own marketing plan relevant to its marketplace. The Marketing or BD Director subsequently produces an over-arching marketing plan for the organization's leadership team.

The essential components of a robust marketing plan include: the management or executive summary, statement of marketing objectives, overview of essential characteristics of the product and market background, the key learnings from the current marketing analyses (in terms of market drivers, threats and opportunities, capability deficiencies, customer issues and competitor pressures), the emerging desired marketing strategy, expected results and benefits to the organization from adopting the plan's recommendations, the marketing programmes required to implement the marketing strategy, required controls and evaluations, financial implications and budgets, information concerning operational knock-on ramifications, plus appendices containing additional details.

The marketing plan must state what is the intended outcome from operationalizing the plan in terms of performance metrics. The focus of the plan should be the details of what must be done, by whom, how, when and at what cost, in order to action the recommended marketing programmes and pursue the desired marketing strategy. To be accepted by the leadership team, the marketing plan should include a cost–benefit assessment.

MANAGING MARKETING PLANNING

Part Four examines the problems most often encountered during the process of marketing planning, when producing the marketing plan and implementing the plan's recommendations. These problems can be categorized according to whether they occur before, during and after marketing planning. Most of these impediments can readily be pre-empted. It is inevitable that barriers to marketing planning emerge, yet these can be remedied so long as they are identified.

- Identifying and diagnosing the blockers to progress.

- Understanding the evolving nature of observed problems in marketing planning.

- Treating the problems.

16

Identifying, diagnosing and treating blockers to progress

There is a range of barriers to successful marketing planning which can occur before, during and after the planning process. Many of these barriers may be pre-empted if managers are forewarned about the dangers they pose. Nevertheless, no matter how well marketing planning is executed, evidence shows that problems tend to occur. Most of these difficulties can be managed with relative ease by proactively tackling the underlying causes. This chapter examines the most common barriers to effective marketing planning and suggests appropriate remedies. It will:

- explain the core barriers to the successful adoption of marketing planning;
- show the reader how to learn from other aspects of marketing management and how best to address likely problems;
- identify the changing nature of the barriers most likely to be encountered;
- explore the potential problems at three stages in the planning process: *before* starting to create the new marketing plan, *during* the process of developing the plan and *after* it is complete, when rolling out the resulting recommendations and marketing programmes;
- suggest pre-emptive measures and remedial activity to address the problems;
- aid the development of an appreciation of how best to diagnose and treat these problems.

16.1 NO MATTER HOW ROBUST THE PROCESS ADOPTED, PROBLEMS OCCUR!

Whether marketing planning is well embedded in the organization or newly introduced, problems occur. Some of these can easily be avoided by planning for the marketing planning activity itself! The first step is to acknowledge that the marketing planning process is both disruptive and resource-demanding. Even once the marketing plan has been produced, a number of challenges remain. The execution of the plan will invariably be associated with difficulties which must be addressed if there is to be a successful outcome. By learning from the experiences of others, those barriers to progress can be minimized or rendered null and void. This chapter aims to outline the most commonly encountered problems and to suggest ways for addressing these 'blockers'.

Organizations use marketing planning to coordinate and control their marketing activities. As has been shown throughout *Marketing Planning*, this is a systematic process involving a range of marketing analyses, the identification of competitive advantage, strategy development, plus the creation and implementation of marketing programmes. The outcome is a marketing plan. However, throughout the process, even once the plan has been agreed, problems may be encountered. Unless these difficulties are addressed, the many acknowledged benefits from marketing planning may remain beyond reach.

Among these benefits are greater awareness of marketing trends, more informed decision making, better communication and coordination within and between organizational functions, improved resource allocation, greater flexibility and responsiveness, and more closely connected marketing strategy and programmes. The most common difficulties relate to leadership, cultural and communication issues, data and other resource shortages, problems with personnel, and ensuring the resulting programmes adequately reflect the analyses and strategy phases of marketing planning.

There is surprisingly little help in the literature available to marketing planners trying to overcome implementation problems. Much of what is available focuses on improving internal marketing and communication, on providing clearer guidance to those involved, and on a more systematic application of marketing principles. This advice aims to provide employees with a unified sense of purpose, so that everyone is pulling together towards the same goal. The problem is that such guidance often fails to directly address other likely barriers. In recent times, some marketing planning experts have developed lists of marketing planning 'pre-requisites' designed to help companies anticipate some of the problems they are likely to encounter.

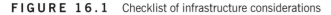

FIGURE 16.1 Checklist of infrastructure considerations

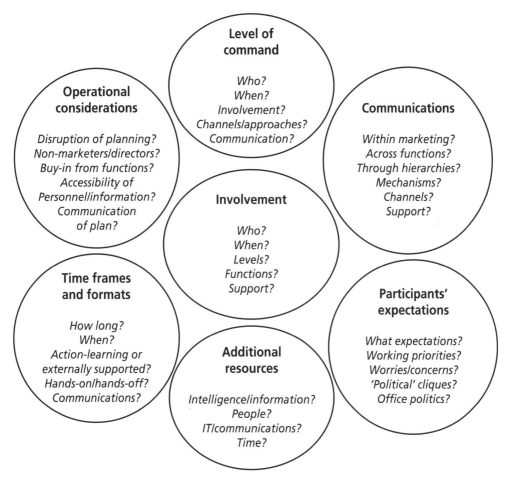

Simkin (2000, 2002a,b) has developed such lists, which cover operational factors, personnel needs, leadership and level of command issues, required resourcing and timing issues, and internal and external communications. These can be used to anticipate marketing planning problems at the earliest possible stage. A proactive approach is then recommended to overcome the problems. Figure 16.1 provides a checklist of issues to consider prior to commencing marketing planning. As explored later in this chapter, consideration of these concerns before the onset of planning helps to limit the problems likely to be encountered.

Implicit in these checklists is the recognition that impediments can arise at different points in the marketing planning process: some are evident at the outset, some occur during the process itself, while others are linked to implementing the planning outcomes.

The barriers or blockers to undertaking and operationalizing marketing planning fall into one of several categories, including:

- the organization's operations, culture and leadership;
- resources and skills available for marketing planning and the roll-out of the resulting plan;
- the marketing information system (MIS) and data;
- communications and coordination within the organization and between parties involved in executing the plan.

These impediments to progress relate to: (i) infrastructure, (ii) process, and (iii) implementation issues. It is important to recognize that problems occur *before*, *during* and *after* marketing planning. See Simkin (2000) and Dibb *et al.* (2008) for a detailed examination of these barriers to successful marketing planning, or Dibb and Simkin (2008) for a discussion of the impediments facing market segmentation.

Even the most rigorous marketing planning processes face barriers. Some of these impediments can be pre-empted by (i) appreciating the likely problems, and (ii) by proactively seeking signs of problems *before* they are allowed to impede progress. Inevitably, there are some problems which can only be tackled as and when they occur. Organizations need to anticipate both expected and unexpected problems and take appropriate remedial action. Failure to do so will allow barriers to progress to operate unchecked, causing the planning initiative untold harm and jeopardizing its viability.

As explored in the authors' book *Market Segmentation Success: Making It Happen!* (2008), too many organizations launch initiatives, new policies or plans which are never properly implemented or used. Subsequent reviews and debriefs of such initiatives reveal the causes of the failure. With hindsight, executives realize that these problems could have been avoided or should have been remedied at an early stage. This chapter explores the most common problems encountered in conducting marketing planning. Using the authors' medical analogy of illness, diagnosis, prescription and treatment, the chapter helps to diagnose the problems, before prescribing a set of practical treatments.

16.2 EVOLUTION OF OBSERVED IMPEDIMENTS TO EFFECTIVE MARKETING PLANNING

In the late 1980s, marketing planning exponent Malcolm McDonald published his views on the most prevalent impediments to the progress of marketing planning. These included a lack of CEO support, little or no plan for the marketing planning activity, along with line management hostility and lack of support, resources and skills. He also noted confusion over technology, jargon and procedures associated with marketing planning, and an emphasis on too much detail in a rigid one-year planning ritual which in many instances amounted to 'planning for the sake of planning'. There was short-hand use of market share and sales figures in lieu of written marketing objectives and strategies. Other observed barriers included the separation of planning from other functional areas in the business, failure to relate marketing planning to corporate planning, and the delegation of marketing planning to planners. More fundamentally, McDonald identified confusion within many organizations between the marketing function and the marketing concept, compounded by a lack of marketing knowledge and skills, plus poor distinction between the marketing planning process and its outputs.

By the mid-1990s, the situation had improved, with more organizations having established marketing functions and seeking to deploy marketing planning. Nevertheless, research by the authors of *Marketing Planning* noted there was still a poor grasp of the marketing concept and few organizations were genuinely market focused. There were significant deficiencies in terms of the marketing analyses undertaken and within organisations' strategizing processes. Strategy was often determined in isolation of any analysis or the formulation of the marketing programmes intended to support the strategy. There was a blinkered view of the external marketing environment, poor and inadequate marketing intelligence, compounded by little internal sharing of available marketing intelligence. For marketing planning, there was inadequate understanding and support from senior management. Procedural problems included poor internal communications within the marketing function and between functions and levels of management. Marketing planning often failed to encourage lateral thinking, so that analyses did not lead to creative updating of strategies. Owing to these problems and the lack of senior support, personnel involved with marketing planning often 'ran out of steam' or were overtaken by events internally or in the marketplace. Perhaps understandably, these managers often exhibited a lack of confidence.

More recent research suggests significant changes in the sorts of barriers encountered by managers executing marketing planning and target market strategies. The marketing concept is now better understood by senior managers and the marketing planning process has become a recognized route to achieving it. The bulk of concerns expressed by marketers involved with marketing planning now relate to (i) communications, (ii) marketing intelligence, (iii) managerial behaviour, (iv) resources, and (v) the necessary alignment of the organization to the resulting marketing plan.

The key blockers to the effective use of marketing planning are now viewed as:

1 inadequate communications within the company;
2 difficulties in harmonizing planning across the organization's locations, business units and target markets;
3 poor assessment of the external marketing environment;

4 insufficient competitor information and customer insights;

5 failure by managers to take a holistic view of the marketplace and its associated challenges;

6 lack of strategic planning skills among senior managers and the inability to objectively interpret marketing analyses;

7 inadequate involvement of non-marketing colleagues and management teams;

8 individual manager's career building at the expense of inputting openly to the planning process;

9 the time available to undertake the required marketing analyses and produce the marketing plans;

10 disruption caused by staff turnover within the team producing and implementing the marketing plan.

Previous concerns about 'what is marketing?' or 'why should we adopt marketing planning?' have been replaced with more practical concerns about process, management and resourcing. The need for viable marketing planning foundations in terms of the infrastructure and adopted process remains, as does the importance of controlling the roll-out of the resulting marketing plan. While the nature of the barriers has evolved, their impact on effective implementation remains a real and serious impediment to the effectiveness of planning and strategizing. These blockers are explored in the remainder of this chapter.

16.3 CORE BLOCKERS IMPEDING MARKETING PLANNING

The most damaging problems hampering the effective use of marketing planning relate to (Dibb et al. 2008):

- *Operations*, *structure* and *leadership* within the organization.

- *Resources* available and the *skills* of those determining the planning strategy.

- The *MIS* and *data* regarding market conditions and the operations of the organization.

- *Communications* within the organization and *coordination* of the planning process.

The impact of each of these areas is discussed in relation to the:

1 *infrastructure* provided for planning – these barriers relate to what is in place '*before*' the planning process takes place;

2 *process* utilized to develop the segments and the target market strategy – these barriers arise '*during*' the planning process itself;

3 *implementation* of the resulting planning solution – these barriers occur '*after*' the output of the planning process has been implemented.

Research by the authors has explored the problems most typically encountered by organizations undertaking and implementing marketing planning. The main blockers reported by practitioners and academic researchers are:

- Ineffective senior management involvement, support and championing.
- Not enough suitably skilled personnel to produce the components of the plan across the business units, product groups or markets necessary, to undertake the marketing analyses, to identify an appropriate marketing strategy and to specify the marketing programmes at the heart of a marketing plan along with a roll-out plan.
- Inadequate creative thinking in terms of interpreting the marketing analyses and their implications for the organization's marketing strategy and when considering the marketing programmes to execute.
- Incomplete marketing analyses, notably in terms of PEST trends of the marketing environment and competitors' strategies. If an organization does not face up to these challenges in its marketing planning, it is unlikely to do so at any other time.
- Ill-defined objectives, presenting problems in agreeing the marketing strategy central to the evolving marketing plan and when rolling out the required marketing programmes.
- Poor planning of the marketing planning process to follow and how best to adopt a viable approach.
- Insufficient topical marketing intelligence, hindering the creation of the marketing plan and the development of the eventual consumer or business customer engagement plan.
- Slow responsiveness to market changes either brought about by the organization's new marketing plan or caused by aspects of the marketing environment.
- Ineffectual tracking of the effectiveness of the deployed plan and poor internal championing of the resulting impact on corporate performance.
- No reviews or remedial actions until next year's marketing planning season!

These problems illustrate the need to address (i) problems that will impact on the organization's ability to conduct marketing planning, and (ii) the problems faced once the planning outputs have been agreed.

16.4 DIAGNOSING MARKETING PLANNING BLOCKERS

Figure 16.2 summarizes the main marketing planning blockers, categorized on the basis of infrastructure, process and implementation.

16.4.1 Infrastructure blockers: the diagnosis

Barriers to planning exist even before the process of creating the plan gets underway. In this section of *Marketing Planning* these *infrastructure* barriers are explored in more detail.

Failure to look forward causes serious problems for companies embracing planning. Even future-oriented organizations can have difficulties, particularly when senior executives fail to understand the scope and impact of the marketing planning process. Such infrastructure blockers can seriously impede the ability to undertake planning activities.

In practice, for most organizations adopting marketing planning, at least some of the senior executives are prepared for a new-look marketing strategy and marketing plan. Even so, these individuals can underestimate the likely consequences in terms of structure, operations and resourcing, or the disruption caused by the planning process. Effective planning requires willing and able leaders to drive on the initiative. The right people with appropriate skills and mentoring abilities must be involved. Strong leadership is needed to allocate aspects of the required analysis, to ease internal communication, and to ensure that bespoke resources are identified. Those managers with relevant market knowledge and skills must be encouraged to contribute to planning, even if this is at the expense of existing duties.

Shrewd management of basic infrastructure elements is also needed. These infrastructure 'building blocks' relate to the availability of data, financial and personnel resources, as well as to requirements for company operations, structure and communication. A robust marketing intelligence system (MIS) is integral to the requirement for adequate data. This should contain reliable and credible topical information about the marketing environment, customers' purchasing behaviour, competition, the organization's capabilities, brand perceptions, corporate performance and resourcing. Often the required level of data is not in place, so remedial improvements are needed. In more extreme cases, organizations lack customer focus and have a poor culture of data collection. These deficiencies will need to be managed in order to reach the 'entry point' of data availability necessary to create a robust marketing plan.

Marketing planning uses many resources: it impacts upon the time and activities of a variety of personnel, often affecting their ability to carry out regular tasks. Collecting information for the marketing analyses can be especially time consuming. The effort required to fill these information shortfalls sometimes deflects from day-to-day responsibilities. The need to

FIGURE 16.2 Diagnosing the core blockers impeding marketing planning

Diagnosis of marketing planning blockers

	INFRASTRUCTURE	PROCESS	IMPLEMENTATION
Operations, structure and leadership	Naïve appreciation of the marketing planning concept and its requirements; Poor senior management involvement and/or lack of leadership: insufficient support for planning and freeing necessary resources; No long-term view of planning's role and the resulting need to modify strategy and to realign resources; Poor general customer focus within the organisation; A fundamental inflexibility and resistance to change within the organisation; Routinely little or ineffective senior management involvement in marketing initiatives; Inadequate marketing or marketing planning expertise or insufficient marketing personnel.	Ineffective senior management involvement slows the process and fails to free-up people or information; No routine practice in the integration of marketing analyses with strategic decisions or marketing programmes; Poor appreciation of the link with corporate strategy goals and marketing planning; The basic marketing planning process is misunderstood or poorly used; Repeated company re-organization and reallocation of key personnel threaten the stability of the process; Inadequate inter-functional, inter-business unit or inter-site buy-in; Inappropriate recognition of budgeting and resource allocation needs for the planning process by senior managers/budget holders.	Poor senior management involvement, preventing proper implementation of planning outcomes; No clarity in responsibilities for implementation; Track record for implementing corporate initiatives and strategies is at best patchy; Erratic and occasional use of reviews/progress audits; Little timely remedial action taken; Lack of performance measures or the recognition that new metrics must be created to reflect the plan's outcomes; Difficulties adjusting to structural changes resulting from the process; Resistance to modifying organizational culture, structure and distribution; Repeated company re-organization, making implementation difficult to achieve; Senior managers ineffective in tackling 'laggard' or resistant line managers; Inflexibility and/or product focus in the distribution system.

(Continued)

Diagnosis of marketing planning blockers

	INFRASTRUCTURE	PROCESS	IMPLEMENTATION
Resources and skills	Poor understanding of marketing planning principles and potential impact on the organization; Little training/orientation for key marketing analysis and planning skills (notably the analyses); Inadequate bespoke financial resources for conducting marketing planning; Insufficient time to plan/conduct the process; Lack of expertise and suitable personnel for analyses and strategic decision-making; Inappropriate allocation of senior managers' time and commitment.	Not enough adequately qualified marketing personnel to undertake the work; Inadequate analytical marketing skills to undertake the required marketing analyses; Insufficient financial resources for the process; Overly-limited data collection and analysis budget; Time taken impinges on day-to-day tasks; Poor knowledge of the marketing planning process and tools; Personnel have inadequate expertise to translate analysis into a meaningful target market strategy and associated marketing programmes.	Insufficient bespoke financial resources needed to implement the resulting programmes; Inadequate re-alignment of resources towards new-look priorities and opportunities; Ineffectual levels of conviction or commitment by the organization's leadership; Time taken to implement the process continues to impinge upon day-to-day tasks; No recognition that roll-out requires appropriate people and time; Failure to factor-in that newly scoped marketing programmes have new requirements, including personnel.
MIS and data	No MIS in place; Inadequate customer buying behaviour data; Lack of competitor intelligence; No analysis of the macro marketing environment trends; Poor appreciation of organizational capabilities and weaknesses; Weak culture of data collection; Ineffective sharing of available intelligence; Ill-informed managers.	Inadequate marketing customer data to update go-to-market offerings and customer engagement plans; Incomplete knowledge of the marketing environment and competitors to select or prioritize opportunities to target; Inadequate analysis skills; Poor efforts to update the MIS and to check the quality of information; Weak culture of data collection and sharing, making it difficult to fill data gaps.	The need to continually update the MIS is not acted upon; No ethos created for routinely using/ adding to the information in the MIS; Ineffective ongoing evaluation of market dynamics and competitor activities; New or revised performance metrics not established; Ongoing monitoring of progress only ad hoc.

(Continued)

Communication and coordination	Weak communication within/between functions, causing problems instigating and deploying marketing planning; Poor identification and awareness of key stakeholder groups; Poor management of required champions; Little inter-functional cooperation; Poor pooling of market insights and marketing intelligence; Inadequate sharing of outputs and creation of new goals.	Weak communication within/between functions impedes efficiency of the process; Information often perceived to provide individuals with power at the expense of others; Poor championing by senior managers; No involvement of the personnel likely to be impacted upon by implementation of the emerging marketing plan; Ineffective orientation to emerging strategic imperatives of the senior leadership team.	Planning benefits not communicated inside the organization; Weak communication within and between functions, causing slow, inefficient implementation; Unclear demarcation of responsibilities for implementation; Poor internal targeting and internal marketing of outcomes/decisions; Leadership team not closely involved with encouraging/policing roll-out; New brand positioning marketing communications ineffectively developed and executed; Identified capability weaknesses not adequately prioritised.

The sentiments within this Figure owe their origins to the authors' experiences with marketing planning (cf: 'Diagnosing and Treating Operational and Implementation Barriers in Synoptic Marketing Planning', *Industrial Marketing Management*, 2008), but echo the implementation problems encountered in creating a market segmentation strategy, as described in the authors' *Market Segmentation Success: Making It Happen!* (Haworth Press, 2008).

Adapted from: S. Dibb and L. Simkin, 'Overcoming Planning Barriers: Four Case Studies', (2001) and S. Dibb et al, 'Diagnosing and Treating Operational and Implementation Barriers in Synoptic Marketing Planning', (2008), both *Industrial Marketing Management*.

include those managers in the process who will be integral to the implementation of the plan's recommendations is a further complication. Resource allocation must be carefully planned to consider all of these issues. If the skills of available personnel are not appropriate, the options are to retrain, hire new blood, or retain consultants with specialist expertise.

There must be free-flowing internal communications and the sharing of information for the creation of a plan and subsequent roll-out of appropriate marketing programmes. This is imperative if the gap between sales and marketing staff and between product groups and segments is to be effectively bridged. High quality analysis is central to good planning practice (see Chapter 1). There must be the provision and pooling of adequate marketing intelligence, the sharing of 'so what?' and 'how about?' ideas, plus agreement on a mutually acceptable way to proceed throughout the planning process. This implies the need for cooperation, which in some organizations is not the norm. In such cases, careful control and orchestration are needed.

16.4.2 Process blockers: the diagnosis

Strong leadership is essential if the planning process is to be effective. This must guide participants and ensure the robustness of the process that is pursued. In organizations operating across numerous sites or territories, or involving many different business units or product group teams, such guidance and control are even more important. Without leadership, managers may take short-cuts and be blinkered in terms of who to involve in the planning, undertaking marketing analyses, opening their minds to the implications from these analyses, revising the marketing strategy as appropriate and being brave in terms of specifying appropriate marketing programmes. 'Bright thinkers' from outside the marketing function can often add a valuable new perspective. Senior managers are responsible for ensuring the plan's recommendations fit well with the company's strategic plan, especially if resources need to be reallocated. In some cases the results of marketing planning will result in changes to this corporate strategic plan. Such changes to strategic direction and resource allocation must be energetically pursued.

A commonly encountered process impediment is that executives fail to identify a suitably robust approach for undertaking marketing planning. The analyses and required market insights will only emerge when the core analyses and their implications have been carefully considered. Managers must often freshen up their thinking if the organization's marketing strategy is to evolve to reflect these insights. The continuation of existing sales and marketing programmes is all too easy for risk-averse managers already pressured by targets. The planning process must therefore facilitate change by ensuring the marketing strategy is appropriately updated.

Planning places high demands on staff, their time and on the organization's financial resources. The allocation of personnel to the process is particularly critical, with managers needing flexibility to carry out and communicate the results of the planning activities. This call on resources is unlikely to be short-lived. Key personnel must be protected to allow them to undertake the essential planning analyses, create the strategy and help steer the subsequent sales and marketing programmes. The necessary analytical skills may be lacking, requiring recruitment or the identification of appropriate third parties to provide the support needed. There may even be a shortage of personnel with basic marketing skills, which would jeopardize any attempt to undertake and implement marketing planning.

At the heart of a well-founded marketing strategy, is a clear understanding of changing customer issues, expectations, buying behaviour and influences, marketing environment forces, corporate performance and competitors. The programmes specified in the marketing plan must reflect targeted customers' behaviour and needs, as well as ensure the company is facing up to the emerging opportunities and threats created by the forces of the marketing environment. The resulting programmes must remedy weaknesses in the organization's capabilities and leverage its strengths. Sadly, many companies are only able to descriptively list their rivals, competing brands and products. It is unwise to determine a targeting strategy, develop brand positionings and formulate marketing programmes in ignorance of competitors' plans and branding. Even when organizations possess adequate marketing intelligence and data, such information may not routinely be shared between operating functions and management teams.

Channels of communications within and between functions must be free flowing, playing a role in providing marketing intelligence, undertaking the analyses, identifying the marketing strategy, agreeing target market and brand positioning strategies, and selecting the appropriate marketing programmes. The implementation process is often smoother if personnel who manage the resulting sales and marketing programmes have been involved in the marketing analyses and marketing strategy phases. They are more likely to take ownership of these planning outcomes if their market knowledge and ideas were taken into consideration. If this cannot be achieved, the robustness and direction of the plan will need 'selling' to these operational personnel and the desirability of the plan's recommendations must be communicated effectively in order to facilitate buy-in and support. These issues should be considered before the roll-out stage of planning, otherwise there may be strong internal resistance by key stakeholders to the proposed changes to sales and marketing programmes.

16.4.3 Implementation blockers: the diagnosis

Robust marketing planning rarely endorses all of the company's existing priorities and sales and marketing programmes. As a result, changes within the organization are often needed during the implementation phase. This will involve adjustments to personnel, budgets, reporting structures and operating systems. Sales personnel, channel management, logistics, advertising and marcomms activities, customer support and dealer handling will all require realignment to reflect the newly created plan. In some cases a complete corporate reorganization and restructuring may be needed to reflect the new priorities and the updated marketing strategy. Careful management and strong leadership at this stage can reduce resistance to such reorganization and operational realignment. Leadership should also ensure that everyone clearly understands their role and the required deadlines for implementing the plan. Lack of such senior championing is a significant blocker to rolling-out the proposed plan.

Just as the people, time, communication and budget resources allocated to marketing planning can prove inadequate, rarely are contingencies made for tackling unanticipated events. Yet unexpected barriers often arise during implementation, requiring time, effort and resources to overcome. For example, there may be resignations because personnel are not prepared to be reallocated. Channel arrangements may be contractually difficult to redefine and realign. The rethinking of brand communications requires time and planning to establish a new positioning in the minds of targeted customers. There must be a sense of purpose and conviction amongst senior executives in order to drive through implementation.

Data requirements are primarily a blocker during the process stage, when the marketing plan is being created. Although these needs may have eased during implementation, progress must be tracked, reporting systems modified and information about targeted customers' perceptions and competitors' reactions collected. There is a continual need to update customer, marketing environment and competitor data. Developments and competitor moves within targeted markets must be monitored and appropriate actions taken to update the marketing strategy accordingly. Judging the effectiveness of the plan and tracking performance in priority target markets are important tasks for ensuring planning success, with data demands that must be addressed.

How well managers are able to communicate the new marketing strategy and programmes is a key factor in determining implementation effectiveness. Communicating these planning outcomes ensures that business units and other managers are made aware of the strategic and tactical proposals. It is wrong to assume that new personnel will automatically cooperate with changes in corporate goals and direction. Senior managers need to carefully coordinate the communication process to maximize the chances of success. Ongoing internal contact must be maintained with the many external agencies involved in customer communication and engagement. If the new marketing plan is to be effectively communicated, individual roles must be clearly specified and responsibilities, reporting lines and timelines for actions well established.

Revising marketing programmes in a marketing planning process has consequences. The necessary skills to operationalize these requirements may be lacking. In particular, the required product, customer service and channel management capabilities may need developing and personnel recruiting or retraining to occur. In organizations with a poor culture of flexibility and acceptance of change, this re-orientation of marketing programmes and realignment of the behaviour of personnel may not be straightforward.

Establishing an appropriate set of performance measures for assessing the impact of the marketing plan is critical to the implementation programme. If the plan has radically reoriented the organization's marketing strategy, it is unlikely that existing measures will be relevant. The way in which information is recorded and reported is unlikely to fit the newly created plan and priorities. In addition to the 'normal' financial performance measures, marketers should assess market share gains within the prioritized target markets, those customers' changing brand perceptions and their levels of customer satisfaction. There may be a realignment of budgets to reflect the revised marketing strategy and marketing plan priorities. In assessing performance and pay-back, the leadership team must be realistic and transparent about the time required to realign the organization's operations, implement the revised marketing strategy, restructure personnel, and modify channel structures, product specification and service levels, pricing policies and so forth. The setting of unrealistic timelines is a common obstacle to effective implementation.

16.5 TREATING THE DIAGNOSED MARKETING PLANNING BLOCKERS

Once identified, the planning impediments must be addressed. Essential treatments for the well prepared marketing planner are many and varied. They include championing, mentoring, induction and providing clear direction; good team selection; auditing of resources and marketing intelligence; communication planning and facilitation; skill gap rectification; data collection and storage; information access; specification of the roll-out, empowerment, timing and resources; setting of performance measures; and progress monitoring and review meetings (Figure 16.3).

16.5.1 Infrastructure blockers: the treatments

At the outset of marketing planning, those driving the process should consider their organization's track record in launching strategy and

FIGURE 16.3 Treating the diagnosed core blockers impeding marketing planning

Treatment of marketing planning blockers

	INFRASTRUCTURE	PROCESS	IMPLEMENTATION
Operations, structure and leadership	Identify and involve a senior champion; Clarify the level of command, empowering those responsible with driving the marketing planning process forward; Establish the requirement for skills and personnel; Recognize and learn from the corporation's previous failures.	Clarify the process and identify key milestones; Identify personnel required for analyzing customers, the market situation, competitors, opportunities and capabilities; Facilitate necessary changes to organizational culture, structure or distribution; Review the ongoing fit with corporate strategy.	Conduct an audit of the organization's track record for implementing planning outcomes, identifying areas of previous difficulty; Develops a specification for implementation and roll-out of necessary marketing programmes, including timescales; required personnel, financial and other resources; reporting procedures; and leadership schedules; Facilitate any required structural realignment and changes to resource allocations; Agree performance measures against which progress will be monitored and when.
Resources and skills	Audit requires financial and personnel resources and compare with those available; Identify shortfalls and develop an action plan to overcome them; Earmark and ring-fence essential resources; Identify teams of participants, ensuring cross-functional involvement as needed; Ensure necessary participant availability by liaising with relevant line managers; Protect the time of key participants.	Identify skill gaps and training needs; Seek external input if necessary; Check ongoing availability of personnel, time, financial and other resources.	Assess the availability of resources for the implementation activities included in the detailed specification, taking action to deal with any shortfalls; Ensure the necessary authorizations are in place to sign-off required personnel, time, financial and other resources.
MIS and data	Review available marketing intelligence against project needs;	Agree priorities for required additional data; Collect data;	Ensure procedures are in place to routinely update the MIS as new data become available;

	Develop a checklist of required data and options for filling these gaps; Ensure there is an adequate MIS set-up, with ready access for participating managers.	Update the MIS as data become available.	Police the quality and frequency of data updates; Assess ongoing competitor reaction and customer response; Establish appropriate performance metrics, collecting the relevant information and sharing these results.
Communication and coordination	Plan and facilitate channels of communication; Create a schedule of reporting points/sessions; Induct participants into the planning process, managing expectations about what will be involved and explain participants' roles within the process; Develop and communicate the timeframes and format for the planning process, so that participants can allocate the required time; Take action to enable required communications between participants and those with whom they must liaise, so that easy access to information and personnel is assured.	Instigate regular internal debriefs of data and ideas; Communicate with internal audiences as the analyses and strategic thinking progress. Ensure appropriate sharing and access to data and key personnel throughout the process; Stage presentations of the resulting plans.	Set up orientation sessions for participating managers and other organizational members to widely communicate the outcomes and implementation needs of the planning process; Ensure senior champions promote the solution; Specify a schedule and the roll-out responsibilities; Develop a schedule of interfunctional and cross-hierarchy review meetings to monitor progress against performance measures, maintain momentum and provide support to overcome operational problems. Establish procedures for remedial actions to handle emerging implementation problems; Communicate subsequent successes in terms of corporate performance and 'wins'.

The sentiments within this Figure owe their origins to the authors' experiences with marketing planning (cf.: 'Diagnosing and Treating Operational and Implementation Barriers in Synoptic Marketing Planning', *Industrial Marketing Management*, 2008), but echo the implementation problems encountered in creating a market segmentation strategy, as described in the authors' *Market Segmentation Success: Making It Happen!* (Haworth Press, 2008).

Adapted from: S. Dibb and L. Simkin, 'Overcoming Planning Barriers: Four Case Studies', (2001) and S. Dibb et al, 'Diagnosing and Treating Operational and Implementation Barriers in Synoptic Marketing Planning', (2008), both in *Industrial Marketing Management*.

marketing. Much can be learned from previous mistakes: the scheduling of the process needs to avoid 'hot spots' in the corporate calendar, and the involvement of personnel who are unlikely to be supportive should be avoided.

The identification of a robust process, involving external support or facilitation where necessary, is a core requirement. Selecting the 'right' personnel to involve in the marketing planning and implementation of programmes, is also critical. Managers with a sound understanding of customer behaviour, market developments and competitors should be involved. Personnel likely to be affected by the eventual plan should also be in the team, as early participation encourages eventual buy in. Sales managers in particular should have a voice in the process. Those managers who will ultimately be responsible for operationalizing the marketing programmes must be included throughout.

A well-respected senior executive should publicly and visibly champion the project. The process can be smoothed by involving the organization's leadership team in assessing the implications from the marketing analyses, in the creation of the revised marketing strategy, and in specifying the core requirements of the associated marketing programmes and resourcing. The leadership team and the project champion must also manage and coordinate communications with the functions, business units and managers involved with and affected by the planning process. There should be an internal orientation programme to engender support and cooperation for the planning and its outputs.

The required financial, IT, analytical, time and human resources must be earmarked prior to the start of planning. Managers who will be involved must be warned, so that they are ready to devote the required time and energy to the process. Marketing intelligence needs – data identification and collection, storage, sharing and validity – should be addressed at the same time.

16.5.2 Process blockers: the treatments

Once actively conducting planning, emerging skill gaps must be quickly rectified, using external support where necessary. External help is often needed to support the collection of customer data or to carry out marketing environment (PEST) and competitor analyses. No organization ever has all of the required information immediately to hand. The information gaps should be prioritized, particularly if planning is a new activity. This may involve the creation of an MIS to capture the customer, market and competitor data required for the early stage of the process.

The overall planning process should be broken down into a series of stages or milestones. Each should have a deadline. When each stage is concluded the team should brief key stakeholders and interested parties about progress to date. At such points in time, emerging problems can be identified, debated and appropriate action taken. Typical problems relate to (i) late or absent buying behaviour, market trend and competitor data, (ii) key personnel being diverted to other tasks or missing meetings, (iii) little involvement and overt commitment from the leadership team, (iv) failure to release budgets for data collection, analysis or MIS management, (v) poor time management and slipping deadlines, (vi) misleading or inadequate communication to colleagues about the project and progress. Being open and honest with colleagues about the problems eases the process of managing and mentoring the project. This is particularly the case where marketing planning is new to the organization.

At agreed points in the process, the planning champion should assess the synergy between the emerging marketing plan and the corporate strategy, stated goals and the expectations of the leadership team. The leadership team must be made aware of any problems of fit between the analyses undertaken, strategy development and programme alignment. Should the evolving planning solution even hint at the need for modified sales and distribution structures, the affected line managers should be canvassed and their expectations gently managed, thus facilitating roll-out of the plan.

Once produced, the marketing plans should be showcased to senior leadership executives and to the business unit line managers to foster commitment and publicly demonstrate appreciation for everyone's efforts. The leadership team may have to make some difficult trade-offs in terms of agreed priorities and associated resourcing. Widespread exposure to the overall marketing plan facilitates acceptance of the eventual resource allocation amongst those managers not receiving everything they had requested.

16.5.3 Implementation blockers: the treatments

Following completion of the marketing analyses, required modifications to the company's marketing strategy must be made. Once the revised marketing strategy, priority opportunities and target markets, required positioning and competitive advantage are agreed, the focus is on developing appropriate sales, marketing, communications and customer engagement programmes. These implications for the organization's marketing programmes must be explained to all personnel who are affected. Experience shows that such internal communication should be treated as a launch programme. The success of the overall marketing planning approach will depend upon shrewd audience selection, clarity of message, emphasis of the benefits and warnings about what will happen if the new plan is not deployed. Involving a credible senior champion during this phase can make a major difference to this process.

Planning solutions inevitably involve a degree of structural and operational realignment, resource re-allocation and reorientation of personnel. Details of these requirements should be communicated to relevant stakeholders and the benefits of the new approach explained. The success of the plan's roll-out can only be assured when (i) resources are explicitly and quickly realigned to reflect the opportunities and priority target markets; (ii) responsibilities and timelines are visibly stated; (iii) adequate time is allocated to create and roll-out the marketing programmes; (iv) competitors' reactions and targeted customers' responses are assessed; and (v) internal performance criteria are redefined to reflect the new marketing plan and activities within each target market prioritized.

A key lesson from previous marketing planning work is the need for formal reviews to assess the effectiveness and appropriateness of the newly devised marketing plan. The core aims of these review meetings are to explore whether operational, resource, personnel or leadership inadequacies are impeding progress and to identify managers who are failing to comply with the new plan's recommendation and marketing programme requirements. Appropriate remedial actions can be specified and taken, but only where organizations proactively identify on-going problems. Such reviews should consider whether the plan or marketing programmes should be changed to reflect market developments. These sessions can also be used by the leadership team to convey appreciation to those responsible for undertaking and implementing the marketing planning process.

SUMMARY

Marketing planning in any organization encounters barriers. Such impediments can be encountered prior to commencing marketing planning, during the planning process itself and when operationalizing the resulting plan and marketing programmes.

The core blockers relate to operations, structure and leadership; resources and skills; the MIS and data; and to communication and coordination. These blockers must be diagnosed and treated if they are to be overcome. Never sit back passively, expecting trouble-free marketing planning! Many of the most common problems can be pre-empted and managers can ensure they are prepared for the unexpected.

Senior managers should proactively seek out and address the inevitable barriers if their marketing planning is to be successful. Having the required conceptual knowledge, marketing intelligence and market insights, together with a suitable process for planning is part of the solution. A sound grasp of the likely organizational and managerial issues is also needed. The problems do not cease once the marketing plan is created: managing the roll-out of the marketing plan is crucial for planning success.

Essential treatments for barriers include championing, mentoring, induction and providing clear direction; good team selection; auditing of resources and marketing intelligence; communication planning and facilitation; skill gap rectification; data collection and storage; information access; specification of the roll-out, empowerment, timing and resources; setting of performance measures; and progress monitoring and review meetings.

No management initiative or strategy execution is ever trouble-free. Marketing planning is no exception. The required investment to create and operationalize a marketing plan is significant. The successful execution of such plans requires that commonly encountered barriers are recognized and treated at an early stage so as to minimize any damage. The guidance in this Part of *Marketing Planning* and the suggested actions are here to help.

PART FIVE

APPLIED ILLUSTRATIONS – CASE STUDIES

Part Five presents a set of cases which illustrate a range of issues associated with the implementation of marketing planning. These cases cover a range of organization types, sectors and sizes.

- Case study 1: JCB's adoption of marketing planning

- Case study 2: Marketing planning and mental health: St Andrew's Healthcare

- Case study 3: Fujitsu planning for the customer's experience

- Case study 4: Marketing planning in an SME: Scope and process issues for Box Technologies

- Case study 5: Managing marketing planning in global operations: InterContinental Hotels Group

17

Appreciating how to undertake marketing planning in practice

CASE STUDY 1: JCB'S ADOPTION OF MARKETING PLANNING

A small lock-up garage in rural Staffordshire producing farm vehicles from wartime scrap metal in the 1940s has grown into a manufacturing and marketing success on a global scale. JCB's award winning, fully landscaped modern production facilities and innovative products continually set new industry standards. There are now ten UK factory sites and manufacturing bases in North America, India, China, Brazil and Germany, eight subsidiary sales companies and twelve regional offices around the world. Following Caterpillar's acquisition of diesel engine producer Perkins, from which JCB used to source its engines, JCB built its own engine plant and now designs its own engines. The World Land Speed record of 563.41 kph recently went to the JCB *Yellow Pencil*, powered by JCB engines! JCB is the fourth largest construction equipment manufacturer in the world and market leader in Europe. With 76 per cent of JCB products exported to over 150 countries, the company is making significant in-roads in the 'back yard' of key American rivals Caterpillar and Case. There are few construction sites without a bright yellow JCB machine. However, the company has extended far beyond construction, into agricultural and now material handling equipment.

Pursuit of new ideas has characterized this success story. JCB created the backhoe loader – the digger seen on most construction sites and at many roadworks – and is world leader in this core product category. JCB brought the first four-wheel steer, four-wheel drive backhoe loader to the market. The JCB Loadall was the world's original telescopic handler, a product found on construction sites, in warehouses, on farms and even at Grand Prix Formula 1 racing circuits. The JCB Robot became the world's safest skid steer, with operators able to climb out without encountering the lifting arms and risk losing their own.

The JCB Fastrac was the world's first high-speed tractor, much sought after by macho-farmers desiring in-field performance and on-road speed. A recent move away from construction equipment has built on the company's knowledge of vehicle construction and hydraulics, with the innovative Teletruk forklift truck. Its Nephron oil filter system means that in JCB tracked excavators, the oil is cleaner when it is drained from the machine than when it was first poured in. There are numerous other examples of leading edge product development, but the take out is that JCB is forward-looking and innovative. This ethos places significant demands on the company's marketers.

Until only a few years ago, the company's founder was still at the forefront of product development and technical innovation. The Bamford family still controls one of the UK's main privately-owned companies. Continued growth is typified by the story of the backhoe digger's evolution and JCB's dominance in this category, along with the reputation of a brand name now part of everyday language. As humorist Miles Kington of *The Independent* newspaper has written:

> I don't suppose the marketing managers of the Roman Empire ever sat down one day and worked out a snappy set of initials, then did some market research on it to see if it was going down well with the people they had just conquered. They just had SPQR on their plates and used it. A bit like JCB. If the man behind JCB had not been called Joseph Cyril Bamford, but something like Patrick James Walker, we would now be saying: 'Look at all those PJWs – they must be building a new road', or, 'Sorry I'm late – I was stuck behind a bloody PJW for five miles down a B road', or, 'Pardon, mais ma voiture fut attrapée derrière un sacré PJW pendant des heures'.

According to management writer Robert Heller, 'JC Bamford, a very British company, is also devotedly international in two powerful senses. In the worldwide spread of its bright yellow machines to 150 different countries, and in its methods. Design-led, aggressively innovative, progressive in its manufacturing and European in its thinking. JCB has consistently raised its global market share in the teeth of world-class competition, while averaging high profitability over a sustained period'.

A large, complex and volatile market

Worldwide the construction equipment industry is huge, with sales close to $70 billion. The US giant Caterpillar tends to concentrate on the very large earthmoving and construction equipment. Similarly, Japanese players such as Komatsu (number two worldwide to Caterpillar) and Hitachi compete for sales of the larger machines. JCB dominates the middle ground, avoiding really heavy earthmoving equipment, but over the past decade the company has made significant inroads into compact equipment and also power tools.

FIGURE 17.1   JCB's main product groups

Backhoe loaders	Tracked excavators
Wheeled excavators	Compact excavators
Wheeled loaders	Agricultural wheeled loaders
Telescopic handlers	Agricultural telescopic handlers
Articulated dump trucks	Rough terrain forklifts
Fastracs	Skid steer loaders
Teletruks	Dumpsters
Micro excavators	Compact tractors
Utility vehicles	Zero turn mowers
Rapid blow tampers	

The company has over 25 per cent of the world's and close to 40 per cent of Europe's backhoe market, led by constant mechanical innovation and improved driver comfort: Case, Ford and Massey Ferguson all trail behind JCB. The JCB brand name is synonymous with this product, often being used as a generic term for the backhoe digger in the industry. Nevertheless, JCB is very much a growing company and the backhoe is only one of many core product areas. More are being added, such as the Teletruk forklift. Recently, a series of machines has been created for military operations. These introductions are based on thorough market opportunity analysis, comprehensive marketing planning and product innovation.

The construction market is highly competitive, and often the victim of economic recession. Whenever there is a dip in spending, economic 'belt-tightening' or a hefty rise in interest rates, the construction industry suffers. This contraction is reasonably regular and must be combated by shrewd planning and effective marketing programmes. In such economic down-turns, civil engineering projects fail to find adequate financial backing, governments suspend capital expenditure and halt infrastructure improvements and house building declines.

Lower numbers of new housing starts have a significant, harmful impact on the market. The purchase of equipment costing anything from £10,000 to £150,000 leads to prudent spending by purchasers, particularly in an economic recession. Product reliability, length of service, after-market servicing and parts costs, versatility in operation, residual operating values when re-sold/replaced, all become crucial issues to the operators of such equipment. These customers range from owner-operator 'one-man' companies, to multi-depot plant/tool hirers, to large construction and extractive companies/contractors (Mowlem or Taylor-Wimpey, for example) which own/hire and operate dozens of machines sourced typically from a variety of manufacturers and plant hirers/contractors.

Selling to the one-person owner-operator is not easy. A high retail price is a real obstacle; access is difficult as generally these customers are 'out on a job', rather than conveniently in an office waiting for a

FIGURE 17.2   Key customer sectors

Agriculture	Airports
Construction	Demolition
Grounds care	House building
Industrial	Military
Plant hire	Ports and terminals
Public authorities and utilities	Quarrying
Rail	Road
Timber forestry	Waste and recycling

telephone call or cold-call sales visit; and their business acumen and sophistication are often limited. Potential per unit profit rewards, though, are very good from sales of construction equipment to these customers. The plant and tool hirers, on the other hand, do not use the equipment themselves, but their customers do. These renters/hirers often have little direct experience of the product or the different manufacturers' offerings: they are steered by the plant hire depot personnel's recommendations and the fleet stocked by a particular hire depot.

At the other extreme, the large construction companies such as Mowlem or Taylor-Wimpey own and hire-in equipment, purchasing from various dealers and manufacturers. These large construction companies may have well-defined purchasing processes and even specialist purchasing managers. The driver or operator is unlikely to be the purchase decision maker or the budget holder in such organizations. This is also true for much of JCB's material handling equipment business, where transport termini and large logistics companies have formalized buying and often specialist managers responsible for selecting suppliers. The agricultural market is very diverse: large farming corporations practise buying centre-led formalized purchasing, but smaller owner-farmed operations behave more like the jobbing builder in the construction market. Each market targeted by JCB exhibits unique attributes.

Marketing ethos

The company has six bespoke dealers operating between them 92 outlets in the UK. Outside the UK there is an extensive array of 550 franchised dealers throughout the world, operating over 1000 depots. In addition, core overseas markets have JCB-owned subsidiaries. These are locally formed companies which oversee local product enhancements, supervise dealers and run marketing programmes oriented to their markets' needs; all carefully orchestrated from the company's Staffordshire base in the UK. Here there are five core operations: *JCB Sales* handling marketing, planning, sales, dealer strategies; *JCB Service* oriented to product support and dealer control; *JCB Finance* offering credit and tax-saving financing packages; *JCB Insurance Services* tailoring policies for construction, farming and plant hire businesses; plus the production operations.

Once product-led and then by the 1970s sales-led, the company now benefits from a carefully integrated sales and marketing function, which liaises closely with the production, finance and service functions. The air of 'entrepreneurial flair' still exists, but now is supported with a host of management skills which have together allowed a family-run business to more than adequately compete with the world's major construction and agricultural equipment manufacturers. Much of the company's success and growth during the 1990s stemmed from the introduction of marketing planning. Today, shrewd planning steers much of the company's thinking and orchestrates its sales and marketing programmes across its territories of operation.

Marketing planning in JCB

Planning and analysis have enabled JCB's marketers to better understand their marketplace. The company has invested heavily in researching its core customer groups throughout Europe, carefully utilizing the strengths of its subsidiaries' personnel in the field. Extensive evaluations of competitors' strengths and weaknesses, their competitive positions and likely strategies have led JCB to successfully pre-empt competitors' thrusts and to quickly establish new product launches in target markets.

Towards the end of the 1980s, the then Marketing Director of JCB studied strategic marketing at INSEAD in France. Upon his return to the UK headquarters of JCB he introduced a formal marketing planning process to the company. Recognizing the cultural diversity and complexity of a global business, the Marketing Director opted to focus initially on the UK in order to explore the ways in which to effectively apply marketing planning in the company. To roll out the process across all of JCB's territories, markets and product groups simultaneously would have been beyond his resources and risked causing too much upheaval within the company as managers aligned themselves to the new remit. At the time, the company had four core product groups, including backhoe loaders and telehandlers, plus some quickly emerging new product categories, such as skid steers and mini-excavators. Each product group had its own set of marketers and so each team produced a marketing plan, addressing only the domestic UK marketplace in year one.

As the marketing planning process was new to the company, external trainers were brought in to establish a stage-by-stage sequence of activities and to provide the company's sales and marketing staff with the required analytical toolkit. As illustrated below, a three-stage process was created, commencing with an Orientation Workshop. This training session overviewed the full process – as explored in Part Two – and addressed the core marketing analysis requirements. Stage two used the outputs from these analyses to consider marketing strategy, targeting priorities, positioning and basis for competing decisions, along with associated marketing objectives. Based on this Strategy Seminar, at which the marketing strategy was decided, the sales and marketing teams went away

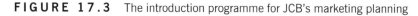

FIGURE 17.3   The introduction programme for JCB's marketing planning

The *A-S-P* programme:

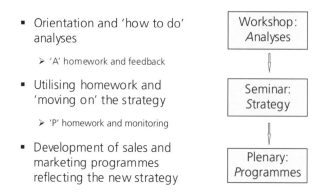

- Orientation and 'how to do' analyses

  ➢ 'A' homework and feedback

- Utilising homework and 'moving on' the strategy

  ➢ 'P' homework and monitoring

- Development of sales and marketing programmes reflecting the new strategy

Workshop: *Analyses*

Seminar: *Strategy*

Plenary: *Programmes*

to formulate their marketing programmes and work plans. These were presented to the full team and senior colleagues during a third workshop, the Implementation Plenary. Any contradictions were ironed out during this session – for example contradictory brand values suggested for different territories or market segments – budgets were prioritized and the company's leadership team signed off the agreed programmes.

Stage one of the process created for JCB included the core marketing analyses: financial performance of the company's products and sales analysis; the marketing environment forces active in each product group's target markets; the buying behaviour characteristics and evolving customer needs; competitors' products, strengths, weaknesses and projected plans; the company's brand positioning vis-à-vis leading rivals; plus an examination of JCB's capabilities.

These tasks proved time-consuming for already busy personnel, so some external support was commissioned in order to research customers and competitors. Nevertheless, the core analyses were all addressed:

- *Marketing environment forces*: *threats and opportunities*. Small teams from within the marketing function were allocated to the different forces of the marketing environment: technological developments, regulatory pressures, economic trends, and so forth. These teams reviewed secondary sources for information, networked with JCB and dealer personnel, met with subject experts to solicit their views, and created a dialogue with industry observers. The emerging issues were discussed and their implications for JCB considered during the first two workshops. Ongoing attention to these issues and emerging threats and opportunities was maintained through quarterly sales and marketing review meetings.

- *Competition*. To examine competitors, the JCB marketers visited trade shows and observed rivals' stands, they reviewed competitors' marketing communications and stated advantages, talked with customers and dealers, analysed rivals' products and marketing programmes, reviewed financial performance and engaged with industry watchers and analysts in order to gain their insights. Customer marketing research benchmarked JCB's brand, products, service, distributors and marketing programmes against competitors' offerings.

- *Customers' perceptions, expectations and purchasing behaviour.* Marketing research in the form of one-to-one depth interviews and focus groups with JCB customers, competitors' customers and JCB personnel, gleaned customers' views of JCB, its products and customer service, changing customer needs and the customers' views of competitors.

- *Capabilities.* Internal brainstorming of JCB's strengths and weaknesses occurred during the first workshop. The outputs were validated and supplemented during the subsequent marketing research, with customer and third party views adding significantly to the internally-generated lists.

Some of these analyses were undertaken by teams of marketers working across JCB's product groups and target markets, while much research was specific to the separate marketing teams handling each core product group in the company.

Within six weeks of the Orientation Workshop taking place, a significant amount of marketing intelligence had been derived, updated, collated and analysed. Stage two, externally moderated by consultants, involved brainstorming workshops with sales and marketing personnel, reflecting on current strategies in the light of the various marketing analyses conducted. As a result, the target market priorities were modified, new products commissioned, revised marketing communications created, modified pricing considered, dealer plans revisited and customer service up-rated. Sales forecasts were revised and the focus of budgets questioned. An important aspect of stage two was the sharing of marketing intelligence, particularly about competitors, opportunities and threats, between the separate marketing teams.

The final stage of the process involved operationalizing the revised/ updated marketing strategy. This roll-out of the strategy required the formalization of appropriate marketing mix programmes, coordination of the separate teams' proposed marketing programmes, plus the allocation of budgets, personnel, schedules and responsibilities to these emerging tasks. Performance measures and review dates were also agreed during the final workshop. An important aspect of the final workshop related to the harmonization of JCB's brand, product and customer service strategies across different JCB product groups, so ensuring that a common approach greeted the individual customer. The size of the task and the market's challenges varied significantly across the company's product groups, with implications for budgeting and resource allocation. These trade-off decisions were made during the final workshop.

Year one had focused on bringing marketing planning to the company's UK product groups. In year two, when the summer marketing planning period was reached, JCB's subsidiary companies overseas were also included, producing top-line marketing plans. Managers overseas were able to learn from their UK colleagues and emulate the format in their resulting marketing plans. For the UK marketers in their second season, there was the opportunity to address outstanding marketing analysis gaps from the previous year and to focus on utilizing the marketing planning toolkit rather than learning about its scope and tools. By year three, the rest of JCB's non-UK operation had become involved, while in the UK the growing understanding of the marketplace facilitated by two years' marketing planning and marketing intelligence gathering led to the creation of newly defined market segments. The marketing plans by year three were segment-specific, ignoring the product groups created by JCB for operational convenience. This led to the formation of the company's Compact Division, which recognized that customers of mini-excavators or mini-skid steers had different purchasing behaviour compared to customers buying the larger-scale versions of such products.

There was a three-year journey for JCB's marketers before the process, core analyses, strategy concepts and joined-up thinking in the programmes rolled-out to customers, fully reflected best practice and met the aims of the company's Marketing Director. There were significant 'wins' in years one and two, with full buy-in achieved in even the most reticent territories by the end of the third annual marketing planning cycle. After three years, one senior manager described the process thus,

> In the first year it was really hard – hell: learning new skills; realising we had inadequate or incomplete knowledge of market trends, competitors and even customers; adjusting to undertaking the planning work alongside our 'day jobs' . . . just finding the time.
>
> The process now is routine: we never miss the opportunity to find out about customer views, examine competitors or discuss market developments with 'those in the know'. We're also much quicker in producing and delivering the marketing plan.
>
> The big difference is that now the company's strategic planning and budgeting are guided by the analyses and market understanding provided by the marketing plan. More to the point, we're selling more machines, in a larger number of segments to more satisfied customers.
>
> Even better, whether in our French subsidiary, Indian plant or American sales office, we're all addressing the market in a co-ordinated manner and everyone is aware of the requirements for effective marketing planning.
>
> But it has taken three years. Finding the time was hard to start with. It did 'hurt' in the first year!

Outcomes for JCB

Even for the company's core product group, backhoes, there have been lessons from the strategic marketing planning undertaken. For example, the indigenous Italian manufacturer FAI (partly owned by Japan's Komatsu) was strong only in its home market and posed a genuine threat in Italy, requiring a different set of tactics to those employed in the UK. The German construction industry has never really used backhoes, preferring instead larger excavators or smaller compact equipment. The opportunities presented by the united Germany and opened-up Eastern European markets, led JCB to develop this market. For backhoes the Scandinavian market is small and sluggish, reflecting local cultural and competitive characteristics not common to the rest of Europe, but presenting a different set of marketing challenges. Through marketing planning, JCB's sales and marketing personnel are well aware of these nuances, modifying their product specifications and tactical marketing mix programmes accordingly.

The Compact Division was treated by JCB in a similar way to Toyota's *Lexus* operation, with bespoke sales and service personnel in dealers, separate marketing campaigns and focused product development. Centred initially around the 800 series of mini-excavators and the single arm Robot skid steer, in recent years the Compact Division has enjoyed range extension of these two product categories, and the addition to the product portfolio of smaller backhoe loaders, wheeled loading shovels and the Teletruk forklift truck. A multi-million pound factory extension at JCB's Hydrapower operation in Staffordshire was required to support the rapid growth of this smaller equipment range and the impact in the marketplace of JCB's Compact Division. Portable powerpacks and a range of hand-held power tools for drilling, cutting, lifting and pumping have been added to the product portfolio.

Marketing planning was not only applied to the company's products. Underlying the success of JCB's machines is a commitment to customer service. With over 220 machines in the range, long-life quality to support, sales in 150 countries and a brand identity inextricably linked with quality and innovation, JCB's aftermarket operation has to be effective and reliable. Dealer engineers are trained to very high standards. JCB's parts – promoted through the *Keep it Genuine* campaign – are well branded and marketed, offering peace of mind to a growing number of users and customers, who in turn find the residual value of their machines is maintained when the time comes to sell the product or trade it in against a new replacement. Downtime caused by product failure is costly and annoying for customers. JCB's UK dealers all stock the core 300 spare parts most commonly required; 265 vans offer rapid and mobile response to customer problems, and the company guarantees a response within four working hours. Dealer personnel elsewhere in the world are similarly committed to solving user difficulties. The company's helicopters and corporate jet have been known to airlift spares for customers in emergencies. Fixed price menu servicing, pleasant customer areas and facilities in dealer depots, plus friendly and proficient service personnel, have added to the impressive customer service provided by JCB. The company's approach was modelled by the Marketing Director on BMW's aftermarket strategy and emphasis on customer service. The JCB Service operation is a major profit contributor for JCB and is branded as strongly as the company's familiar bright yellow machines.

QUESTIONS FOR DISCUSSION

1 What operational and organizational barriers faced the introduction of marketing planning within JCB?

2 How did JCB's Marketing Director address these potential barriers to progress?

3 What were the core ingredients for the success of marketing planning in JCB?

4 In the context of the complexity of this company and the diversity of its markets, what are the principal benefits from adopting the marketing planning process?

CASE STUDY 2: MARKETING PLANNING AND MENTAL HEALTH: ST ANDREW'S HEALTHCARE

A distinctive healthcare provider!

Mental health problems are far more common than many realize: during their lifetime one in every three people will talk to their doctor about an emotional or psychiatric problem. While for many these difficulties will be temporary, for others more specialist care and support will be required. One in ten people will consult a psychiatrist in their lifetime and one in twenty will be admitted for mental health care.

St Andrew's Healthcare is a not-for-profit charity and a leading provider of independent sector mental health care. St Andrew's Healthcare is not part of the UK's National Health Service (NHS). However, with over 90 per cent of its patients referred by the NHS, there is a close relationship between the two parties. From its 1838 origins as Northampton's prestigious Victorian asylum, St Andrew's Healthcare has diversified into a wide range of aspects of mental health care and now has inpatient units in other parts of the UK. The organization has built a strong reputation for the quality and diversity of its specialist assessment, treatment and rehabilitation services. These range from high quality short-term acute services to secure treatment programmes offered to people with highly challenging behaviours.

Other providers of mental health care, notably private sector operators, have tended to focus on the more lucrative or more readily treatable forms of mental health problems. While such operators often offer only a limited range of care pathways for certain types of patients, St Andrew's Healthcare provides a much more comprehensive range of care. The organization has an enviable reputation as a high quality specialist provider, handling the most complex and challenging behaviours, as well as more mundane and less extreme behaviours. This creates many challenges for the organization's budgeting and capital investment decisions. Men, women and children are catered for in St Andrew's Healthcare, for needs in mental health, learning disability, brain injury and neurological impairment.

A growing income now over £100 million per annum, multiple sites to manage and market, highly divergent patient groups and associated care pathways, complex purchasing dynamics, 2000 specialist employees, along with many capital investment commitments, place significant pressure on the management team. St Andrew's Healthcare is faced with an increasingly competitive marketplace and changing purchasing priorities within the NHS. To address these pressures, a few years ago the organization's CEO turned to marketing planning in order to assist with decision making and resource prioritization.

An enviable reputation

Although a charity, the focus of this organization is not on helping mental health sufferers in the community, or charity shop-style fund raising, or increasing the general public's awareness of mental health issues: other charities and bodies address these important tasks. St Andrew's Healthcare operates several leading-edge facilities, employing acknowledged experts, developing state-of-the-art care pathways and establishing an eminent reputation within the mental health care profession. Different business units address everything from adolescent learning difficulties through to major behavioural problems, with many patients requiring secure accommodation and lengthy treatment programmes. There is a specialist unit dealing with brain injuries and, through an on-site partner, also clinic facilities for patients needing to 'dry out'. An underlying corporate value is that the organization is committed to providing exceptionally high standards of patient care, with an emphasis on ensuring each patient receives and responds to a programme of individual expert treatment.

The brand reputation of St Andrew's Healthcare is based on the quality of its care and the range of care pathways that have been developed, many of which pioneer new treatment approaches. The range of care pathways offered by the organization is an important differentiator against competing providers, but also is of significant benefit to patients.

FIGURE 17.4   The specialities (business units) of St Andrew's Healthcare

Men's services (mental health and learning disabilities)
Women's services (mental health and learning disabilities)
Adolescent services (mental health and learning disabilities)
Brain injury rehabilitation service
Services for older people
Huntington's disease service
Dementia and challenging behaviour service
Acute psychiatry (including eating disorders and addictions)

For example, a patient with severe and multiple problems will be treated on one care pathway, and when improved passed onto another of the organization's pathways. While operated by a separate business unit, the patient nevertheless will remain at the same location, merely moving wards. This is less unsettling for the patient and his/her family. More often than not, competing institutions hand over the patient to the NHS funding body once the care pathway it manages has been completed, with inevitable disruption for the patient, family and those managers in the NHS responsible for the case. This is because competing institutions rarely provide the full range of pathways required to address all situations. The St Andrew's Healthcare brand is built on its ability to relate to patients, their families and to the medical staff or personnel in social services who refer patients to the organization's inpatient units.

Corporate objectives

St Andrew's Healthcare has charitable status, but sets its fees at a level that permits it to provide the high quality care at the core of its ethos. With no shareholders, the organization reinforces its financial success by reinvesting in new developments and improved patient care. The latest major projects have been the new Adolescent Learning Disability Unit and the new Women's Unit. Despite its success, the diversity of operations places significant demands on the organization's capital spending. Wards and facilities require modernizing, newly devised care programmes may require remodelled facilities, the expansion of demand caused by reduced state provision of mental health facilities drives the organization's caring professionals to provide expanded facilities, plus the staff are ideas-led and continually seek permission to tackle more challenges in innovative ways.

Private sector commercial businesses have entered the more financially lucrative parts of the market. St Andrew's Healthcare must defend its position in these segments, as fee income from these activities is required to support the organization as a whole and to cross-subsidize other segments of the market deemed less financially attractive by new entrant competitors.

In order to defend its market share in these segments, the organization has to develop marketing strategies and devote resources to marketing programmes designed to maintain the loyalty of referring GPs, clinicians, support workers and funding agencies. Increasingly it is necessary to tailor marketing messages to a growing mix of audiences. Commercially minded competitors are developing 'glitzy' marketing programmes and St Andrew's Healthcare has to maintain its visibility to key stakeholders in this quickly evolving marketplace.

Complex purchasing dynamics and audiences

While some patients deal directly with the charity, the vast majority of patients are referred from the National Health Service. St Andrew's Healthcare has a reputation for being able to deal with difficult patients suffering with complex problems. However, the NHS is increasingly moving towards centralized buying, with numerous regional Trusts joining forces in order to be able to purchase services – such as those offered by St Andrew's Healthcare – at lower best value rates.

In addition to medical staff diagnosing the patients' problems and recommending appropriate courses of treatment, the NHS has risk assessors, financial managers and professional purchasing executives, who are all involved in the decisions concerning which treatment programme to purchase and from which provider. There are many decision makers and influencers involved in the buying centre. For St Andrew's Healthcare and other suppliers to the NHS, such formalized purchasing and group decision-making complicate the marketing activity and the engagement programmes targeted at key stakeholders.

For the patient, his/her family, the referring medical staff and for the numerous administrators involved, St Andrew's Healthcare must develop bespoke messages, marketing communications and client handling programmes. This complex buying centre must be addressed to allow St Andrew's Healthcare to operate with full bed occupancy and in order to fulfil its mission to help those suffering with mental health problems.

Marketing planning in St Andrew's Healthcare

St Andrew's Healthcare has responded to these market forces by updating its corporate strategy and by developing an associated marketing strategy. It has also allocated resources to producing and implementing marketing programmes. In addition, the organization has recruited business managers to support the various business units' marketing activities. Marketing planning is an important foundation for many of these activities.

Each business unit has a Clinical Director and a commercial manager. They work in close harmony to develop a marketing plan and budget, request capital investment and continually enhance care pathways. The various commercial managers from the many business units are accountable to the organization's Director of Strategic Development, who leads on marketing planning. The units' Clinical Directors report to the CEO for St Andrew's Healthcare. As a psychiatrist with an MBA, he has a sound appreciation of the commercial imperatives emerging through the marketing planning activity, as well as the fundamentals of specialist healthcare.

St Andrew's Healthcare introduced marketing planning via a series of workshops for the clinical heads and commercial managers of the various business units. Members of the leadership team, including the CEO, attended these orientation, training, brainstorming and strategizing sessions. The essential marketing analyses outlined in Part Two were introduced during these workshops. The Clinical Director and commercial manager from each business unit worked jointly with their line managers to populate these analyses and validate their inputs. Each business unit considered market drivers and the PEST forces of the marketing environment; SWOT implications; changing customer needs, buying processes, influencing factors and the complexities of the buying centre; competitors' strategies, the organization's basis for competing and brand positioning. These insights informed the strategy stage of marketing planning, at which emerging opportunities were assessed and priorities determined using the directional policy matrix (DPM). Having agreed which priorities to pursue, appropriate target market strategies and brand positionings were specified. Later in the process, suitably relevant marketing programmes were specified in order to roll out the business units' strategies.

Each business unit used the process to articulate its desired product and service developments, required care pathways and necessary stakeholder engagement programmes. As in all organizations, the overall budget was not sufficient to support all of the business units' marketing plan recommendations. In parallel to the business unit activity, the overarching themes from the analyses of external market drivers, competitors' approaches, customer issues and capability considerations were synthesized by the leadership team of St Andrew's Healthcare. Some tough decisions were then needed in relation to the allocation of resources. The organization's overall opportunity and threat assessment, capability analysis, examination of competitors and new entrants, plus evaluation of brand standing vis-à-vis key audiences, led to a set of well-informed trade-off decisions by the leadership team. The agreed attractiveness criteria and their respective weightings from the directional policy matrix added objectivity to this budget allocation. As a result, some business units each year have their funding and marketing programme requests fully supported, but others must wait or operate with less than requested.

Outcomes in St Andrew's Healthcare

The Adolescent Secure mental health service is a purpose-built development creating new standards in medium secure care for adolescents with challenging mental health needs. This service is for boys and girls aged 13–18 from across Britain, supported by a multi-disciplinary team offering emphatic, safe and therapeutic response to disturbed behaviour, trauma and distress. The facilities required a substantial multi-million pound investment, to provide five residential sub-units designed to accommodate young people with differing needs. The facilities are only part of the deliverable. Well qualified and expensive personnel are necessary to provide the expert assessments and care pathways. In order to justify these investments, bed occupancy must be high, resulting in required investment in marketing communications and the nurturing of diverse relationships within the buying centre.

For the Adolescent Secure Learning Disability business unit, marketing planning led to the creation of Malcolm Arnold House. This is a recently constructed four ward/44-bed facility for 11–18 year old disadvantaged children and young people. These are patients with mild to borderline learning disabilities, challenging behaviours and mental health problems. Expert personnel are required to assess and care for these patients. Owing to the nature of target audiences and buying centre composition, bespoke marketing programmes are again required to ensure full utilization of Malcolm Arnold House.

These advanced adolescent services owe their funding to the marketing opportunity and capability analyses at the heart of the marketing planning activity. To support their investment requests, the Clinical Directors and commercial managers of both business units supplied the leadership team of the organization with robust business cases. Centrally, the market insights provided from the combined business unit marketing plans have helped inform decision making and establish a market oriented perspective to strategic planning in St Andrew's Healthcare. In a highly unusual environment, marketing planning is helping guide a fast-moving and well respected organization to address the many challenges in its marketplace and to make best use of its resources.

QUESTIONS FOR DISCUSSION

1 For what reasons were the analyses of the marketing environment and competitive arena so important to the marketing planning in St Andrew's Healthcare?

2 The marketing planning activity was not left to the marketing personnel or business managers in St Andrew's Healthcare; clinicians and support staff were also involved. Why?

3 In a not-for-profit organization, why undertake marketing planning?

4 Compared with Coca-Cola or Ford, how is undertaking marketing planning in St Andrew's Healthcare different? What are the similarities?

CASE STUDY 3: FUJITSU PLANNING FOR THE CUSTOMER'S EXPERIENCE

IT services

EDS, IBM, HP and Fujitsu are four of the biggest global providers of IT services. Japanese-based Fujitsu, formerly ICL in the UK, is the only non-American in the top ten. Other leading players in the UK include Accenture, KPMG, CapGemini, BT and CSC. The market is led by leading management/IT consultancies and big technology companies. Within specific market sectors there is also a plethora of successful niche players specializing in only that sector or in one service application. To add to this complexity, the standard strategy textbook view of 'beating' competitors does not really apply, as each competitor is likely elsewhere to be a strategic partner or supplier. For example, for one contract IBM may be bidding against Fujitsu, while for another, Fujitsu may be a supplying partner to IBM or vice-versa.

The IT services industry tends to group clients into trade sectors. For example, one leading player has separate business units dealing with Government, Public Sector, Health, Manufacturing, TelCo (telecoms), Retail, Financial Services, Hospitality (hotels, bars, entertainment venues), Travel (train, air, holiday operators – mainly booking systems), and Utilities. All of the leading players adopt a similar approach, employing industry specialists to supplement their own understanding of client drivers in each targeted sector.

Traditionally, IT services companies have sold into CIOs or COOs. The bigger clients will often be using the services provided by a handful of different IT companies. After winning one piece of business in a client, the aim of the IT services company is to spread virally by building links within the client and increasing knowledge of other emerging IT opportunities. More recently, CapGemini, Fujitsu and Accenture have been targeting CEOs, in order to 'move up the foodchain' of client decision making.

The work undertaken by IT services providers falls into four areas:

1 Staple IT services. Desktop outsourcing (management/upgrading of a client's PCs/laptops), call centre outsourcing (to a third party that is expert in offering only this service), data warehouses (large warehouses crammed full of servers, storing many clients' management information and e-mail traffic), are the three largest services. Mobile office solutions (handheld screens, in-car technology, wireless working, etc.) are up and coming. The big outsourcing deals – where a company such as E-On or GM hands over its in-house IT department to Accenture, Fujitsu, BT or IBM – often fall in these areas.

2 All of the major players have developed proprietary products/ services, which are offered across market sectors. For example,

Fujitsu's *Sense & Respond* service is designed to manage clients' call centres. This offering is able to analyse the nature of the complaints being received by a call centre and suggest a required remedial action. The result is that the particular cause for customer complaint is removed and calls to the call centre reduced. IBM meanwhile has majored in e-commerce and 'on-demand' maximizing capacity utilization, by offering clients 'spare' data storage or call centre provision that kicks in only when there is a surge in demand.

3 Each major player focuses on a different set of market sectors, developing offerings focused only on one client group, such as supply chain management for retailers or branch optimization for retail banking clients.

4 Different players respond to specific requests from key clients. For example, the CEO of a large grocery retailer recently said something along these lines:

> Instead of consumers putting a pound into the shopping trolley, if they placed their loyalty card in a slot we'd know who they were before they shopped. We could then have little LCD screens – jumbo-jet style – on their trolleys, tailoring promotional messages and recipe ideas to that individual customer's tastes. In-store, big plasma screens could receive wireless signals from the trolley so that other customized messages could be played to separate customers as they pass by the screens at the ends of aisles or above chiller cabinets. At the till, bespoke vouchers and offers could be ready printed to hook these customers for a return visit. Who can give us these components as a complete solution?

Needless to say, several big IT services companies are already respond-ing to this request for support. Yet an individual IT company is unlikely to have all of the products and capabilities required to service the retailer in the above example. While one organization might have the necessary database analytical skills required to profile customers' spending patterns, another player will have the wireless technology, with yet another providing the LCD and plasma screens, or modifying the EPoS systems at the checkout. The result is that a consortium will often be formed, under a lead partner such as IBM or Fujitsu.

Marketing planning in Fujitsu

When Fujitsu Services (FS) was faced with the challenge of updating its market offerings, the company decided on an innovative approach to the problem, led by its European management team. Its actions were fuelled by the desire to engage with a broader and more senior set of client decision makers, offering IT solutions pertinent to these execu-tives' imperatives. At the heart of Fujitsu's strategic marketing planning is its *Go To Market* process. This adheres to the best practice principles of marketing planning, as explored in Part Two. The basis for the strategic recommendations is an extensive programme of analysis. Suggested client engagement programmes have to reflect the outcomes of these analyses and play to the agreed strategy, in true *ASP* fashion. Otherwise Fujitsu's *Go To Market* process does not approve budgets or schedule the proposed marketing programme activities.

An illustrative example of this process is one of the company's over-arching initiatives, to focus on helping to manage the experiences of clients' consumers, known as its *Customer Experience Programme*. An experienced marketer was assigned to amalgamate a set of 'products' that could be marketed under this banner. The aim was to enable Fujitsu's clients in various sectors to better engage with and look after their consumers, so enhancing their consumers' experiences. In so doing, consumer satisfaction improves, complaints fall, customer churn diminishes (the rate of losing disassociated consumers), clients' brand standing improves and their cross-selling opportunities are facilitated. All of which improves shareholder value for clients' CEOs. In this manner, key strategic drivers for Fujitsu's clients are addressed, through enabling and thought-leading IT.

The under-pinning commercial logic of this initiative is clear. Through this programme clients would reduce the numbers of lost consumers, increase the share of consumers' spending and enhance consumers' perceptions of their brands. For Fujitsu, more business would be won from existing clients, but also the compelling nature of the proposition would appeal to new clients across many sectors. Over time, Fujitsu would become recognized as the organization that helps clients grow their businesses by improving the experiences they deliver to their consumers. More specifically, the *Customer Experience Programme* has the potential to provide Fujitsu with a window into the views of key influencers and decision makers inside carefully targeted client companies.

In a sprawling corporation such as Fujitsu, a significant challenge was to identify a place to start! In common with most technology businesses, another challenge was to be led by clients' market drivers and priorities rather than the organization's own technologies and in-house new product ideas. A team was assembled from across Fujitsu's business units populated by managers familiar with client sector issues and the services currently being offered. It quickly became clear that Fujitsu already had many products and services that were relevant to the *Customer Experience Programme*.

For example, *Sense & Respond* diagnoses consumers' gripes with client companies, so helping to improve these consumers' experiences. The Fujitsu Retail business unit works with many blue chip retailers to evolve the in-store consumer experience and these retailers' on-line services. For Utilities, Fujitsu's *SellSure* enables seamless and painless switching for consumers changing energy suppliers. The Travel business unit provides airport, train and coach clients with information, query handling, ticketing and booking systems. The TelCo business unit supports mobile phone clients with in-store solutions, kiosks, helpdesks and retail solutions. Other examples were found across Fujitsu's many business units.

In order to achieve its objectives and make the planning process manageable, those responsible for the marketing planning programme for the *Customer Experience Programme* followed these key steps:

- *Identify clients' clients/customers/consumer segments.* Starting in sectors with which Fujitsu already had knowledge and links, to build on existing credibility.

- *Survey these clients' and their consumers' experiences.* From the consumers' perspective and from the view of those servicing them, to understand what help to offer and provide added value consumer insights for client Directors.

- *Prescribe solutions.* All aspects of service delivery, not 'just' IT, otherwise the consumers' experience will not be improved adequately.

- *Identify where IT can help.* Whether or not Fujitsu currently has the required capabilities was ignored, to avoid constraints on the propositions developed.

- *Rectify inevitable Fujitsu capability gaps.* Develop in-house capabilities/products and partner with other suppliers, in order to have a plausible story to tell and desirable propositions to offer.

- *Develop a prospect list.* Based on the analyses and emerging propositions to take to market, addressing the most senior pertinent client personnel.

- *Create/recruit a suitable Fujitsu team credible in this space.* Ensuring that Fujitsu has the right sorts of personnel for these clients, with appropriate skills and standing.

- *Develop messages and campaigns.* Make sure that the marketing programme is rolled out.

The real challenge was to offer more than a 'patchwork quilt' of *ad hoc* solutions within the sphere of Customer Experience. In order to succeed commercially, it was necessary for Fujitsu to provide valuable insights to client CEOs and Directors about the nature of their consumers' experiences and how these could be enhanced through innovative IT solutions. Fujitsu adopted a far-sighted approach, investing in qualitative marketing research designed to explore consumers' views in sectors served by their clients. In this way Fujitsu developed deep insights into the needs, wants, expectations and experiences of key clients' customers. Although this research was expensive, the insights it provided were valuable. Now Fujitsu could leverage its new understanding, which clearly differentiated it from competitors, to refine the solutions offered to clients. On the basis of the consumer insights it gained, a series of product development and client engagement programmes were developed as part of the marketing plan.

QUESTIONS FOR DISCUSSION

1 What are the 'unusual' aspects of the market for IT services that add to the complexity of marketing planning?

2 In terms of the *ASP* marketing planning process, which stage was the most important in the formulation of the *Customer Experience Programme*?

3 In executing its *Customer Experience Programme* what operational barriers had to be overcome by Fujitsu?

4 In the context of these market dynamics and operating structures, as Marketing Director for Fujitsu how should marketing planning best be managed?

CASE STUDY 4: MARKETING PLANNING IN AN SME: SCOPE AND PROCESS ISSUES FOR BOX TECHNOLOGIES

Box Technologies is an SME based in Oxfordshire, focusing on offering retail systems and tills to retailers in the UK. Through an enviable set of partners, Box supports national/regional retailers and hospitality companies with leading-edge systems and updates to their on-site technology. Box Technologies works with a carefully selected portfolio of manufacturers in order to provide clients with robust and cutting edge solutions. Elo TouchSystems, Epson, Motion Computing, Metrologic and VeriFone, are just some of these vendors.

Box installs full systems or upgrades existing systems to fulfil clients' requirements and offers full service back-up. The company is a distributor of bespoke EPoS solutions to retailers, pubs, banks, restaurants and entertainment venues. Box is not a manufacturer, instead putting together project solutions/integration, IT systems/computing and in-store equipment for retailers and hospitality companies.

Established in 1992, the original founder sold out to two colleagues who together with four function heads form this SME's leadership team. The company still adheres to the founder's objective, to be a one-stop hardware distributor for European customers in retail and other service sectors. Although primarily focused on hardware technologies through partnerships with software developers, total solutions are provided to client companies. Box Technologies operates a consultative approach to the selection of appropriate hardware, software and networking systems for retail and hospitality clients, based predominantly around tills, EPoS, Chip & PIN and mobile computing products. Indeed, Box describes itself as Europe's 'premier EPoS hardware distributor' with 'an unparalleled track record of systems deployment throughout the retail and hospitality market'.

Box customers

Londis convenience stores, Athena cards and pictures, discounter Poundland, Elf forecourts are some of the typical customers served by Box Technologies. The company's key customer sectors include:

- speciality (non-food) retailers;
- food/C-stores;
- hospitality (restaurants, bars, etc.);
- leisure (hotels, visitor attractions, etc.);
- banking (Forex, retail banking, building societies, the Post Office);
- transport (termini and boats, trains, planes).

Leading concerns for such customers are payment processes, security, self-service facilitation, stock control and supply chain efficiency, all of which are enabled with today's IT systems. These customers often want cost-effective use of technology to reduce staff while keeping their consumers happy. A beguiling array of technology and systems is available to help solve these retailers' and hospitality companies' operational needs. Few companies have the time, money or management resources to adopt everything that is on offer. Box Technologies 'brokers' an appropriate solution from an array of manufacturers for an individual client's specific requirements and commercial situation.

Changing technology

To consumers the use of technology in restaurants, bars, cinemas, banks, retailers or other service providers is now common place. Some examples include:

- at-pump self-payment for fuel;
- self-check registration in hotels or at doctors' surgeries;
- touch-screen catalogue ordering in Woolworths or Argos;
- product/tariff information and query kiosks in mobile phone shops;
- self-service ticketing machines in transport termini;
- thumb print payment recognition in The Co-Operative's supermarkets;

- self-scan and pay checkouts in Tesco;
- at-table touch and order hand-helds for restaurant waiting staff;
- in-queue hand-held ordering at McDonald's;
- library access systems;
- leisure club membership card swipes;
- in-store television and displays.

Most consumers are now familiar with these examples of how technology impacts upon the delivery of services, access to information and payment systems. Perhaps the most visible use of such technology in recent years has been the introduction of Chip & PIN payment systems at tills, designed to reduce the levels of fraud. This is just the tip of the iceberg. Behind the scenes, but not visible to consumers, many aspects of everyday trading life are enabled by technology. For example, stock ordering and replenishment in retailers is heavily automated, meal preparation in restaurants is orchestrated by e-ordering, staff access within secure zones and employee working monitoring are IT-facilitated.

Many of the above developments are very recent. By the time this book is printed, there will be many more. For Box Technologies, such rapid change and the seemingly never ending introduction of new systems and techniques provides a steady stream of clients requiring support or upgrades to their existing systems. Such good news for Box Technologies is tempered by the fact that this small business has to work particularly hard to stay abreast of market developments. The company must also carefully select the areas and technologies on which to focus if it is to continue its effective support of its retail and hospitality customers.

The company's reputation

Market feedback reveals that clients perceive Box Technologies to know products well and understand related customer issues. Customers believe Box offers a flexible, service-led proposition that demonstrates professionalism and commitment to its customers. These are important traits in a market where clients need to be able to trust their technology suppliers and often turn to companies like Box as impartial brokers. In addition to offering impressive product/service levels, the company is viewed as a committed, empowered 'can-do' set of problem solvers who know what product solutions its business customers need. Within the leadership team there is a driving enthusiasm to create a successful business that is attractive to clients, suppliers, partners and employees.

Despite its market standing and impressive client base, Box Technologies depends heavily on its six-strong leadership team and has to stretch its resources in many directions. As well as addressing business growth and considering how best to retain existing clients, the leadership must strive to remain topical and protect its networks with suppliers and partners. There are many other 'distractions' for such a busy team of Directors:

- staff recruitment, retention and training;
- inventory management productivity;
- the search for new premises for such a go-ahead organization;
- on-site health and safety regulations;
- data protection regulatory requirements;
- employment law and working practice regulatory compliance;
- Financial Services Act addressing pensions, liability provision and so forth;
- assessment of market entry into emerging markets;
- banking and taxation requirements;
- brand building, corporate affairs and investor relations.

Marketing planning

Against this busy and challenging set of issues, the Directors of Box wished to use strategic marketing planning to validate the company's sense of direction and agree priorities for the next couple of years. Two directors had previously produced marketing plans, alongside annual budgeting decisions, based on their MBA training. As the company was growing and addressing a broader set of target markets, more formalized planning was necessary. The handful of specialist marketers, sales and business development staff did not have the necessary free time or resources to fully 'own' the marketing planning process. In common with many SMEs, only a few senior executives had an over-arching under-standing of the company's fortunes and knowledge of the company's markets and intended strategies. These directors had to be involved with the company's planning activity, yet they were busy people with many other tasks on which to focus.

The Managing Director decided to progress the key marketing plan-ning stages using an external facilitator to manage several brainstorm-ing workshops. During these sessions the stages outlined in Part Two were addressed. As explored in Part One, the marketing planning pro-cess had to include an assessment of market trends and drivers, emerg-ing opportunities and threats, the organization's capabilities and deficiencies, plus an assessment of what constitutes a worthwhile opportunity. Two workshops focused on these issues and considered the target market strategy needed to pursue the emerging opportunities. The agenda for the first workshop considered the following:

- market trends/developments to address;
- opportunities to pursue;
- competitive threats to counter;

- capabilities to leverage;
- development of a strong basis for competing;
- creation of a compelling brand proposition;
- clear target market prioritization;
- weaknesses to remedy;
- specification of definable objectives.

A break of a couple of months enabled some of the emerging market challenges to be more fully considered. Gaps in the analyses from the first workshop were also filled during this period. A second workshop then addressed the following issues:

- new propositions reflecting the outputs from the analyses;
- Box capabilities;
- Box branding;
- Box weaknesses;
- emerging 'big picture' strategy options;
- required audit of HR practices;
- attractive/worthwhile customers and opportunities defined by the DPM technique.

Box Technologies divided up the required tasks among its senior executive team. For example, the opportunities identified and 'screened in' by the DPM criteria focused on 15 or 16 customers. These were allocated to three of the directors and two senior line managers for ongoing evaluation and contact. Box's ethos, capabilities, brand values and forward thinking are attractive to leading designers, analysts and technologists who have retail and hospitality company clients. In turn, these players could promote Box and network Box with their clients. In this respect, retail designers are key targets for Box Technologies, but so too are retail analysts, journalists and technology experts. Time spent by the Box leadership team with these personnel is an opportunity cost, but such links potentially lead to new business. Two directors agreed to further explore possible links with these parties. Many other marketing plan actions were similarly allocated to one or two key managers.

A major problem for this SME's marketing planning was the shortage of 'spare' personnel and other resources. Progress might have been easier if there had been a team of marketers available to conduct the analyses, undertake the networking and provide the necessary insights into the market's dynamics. Nevertheless, the drive and enthusiasm in Box Technologies – in common with other entrepreneurial SMEs – carried the company through and maintained momentum. While some short-cuts were needed, the team was able to harness this energy so that the core marketing planning stages were addressed.

The nature of the organization meant it was vital to involve the entire leadership team in creating the marketing plan and owning the recommendations. There had to be realism regarding timeframes and coverage of the plan. Junior colleagues were involved and encouraged to 'step up' to more demanding challenges. Certain analytical and strategic planning skills had to be developed and supported externally. Nevertheless, despite the shortfall in personnel resources, this SME found it was possible to use and capitalize upon the principles of marketing planning. Box is not alone in this regard, with many other SMEs now routinely adopting marketing planning ideas.

QUESTIONS FOR DISCUSSION

1 Outline ways in which marketing planning is applied in an SME such as Box Technologies.

2 For Box Technologies, which matters most in marketing planning: analyses, strategy or marketing programmes? Why?

3 What are the pros and cons of involving directors in marketing planning?

4 Would you rather manage marketing planning in Box Technologies or in a larger organization such as Epson or IBM? Why?

CASE STUDY 5: MANAGING MARKETING PLANNING IN GLOBAL OPERATIONS: INTERCONTINENTAL HOTELS GROUP

InterContinental Hotels Group is the world's largest hotel group, with 3650 hotels and over 540 000 guest rooms, in nearly 100 countries. Leading brands within the company's portfolio include InterContinental, Crowne Plaza, Holiday Inn and Holiday Inn Express. With 28 million members, the company's *PriorityClub* is the largest hotel loyalty scheme. InterContinental Hotels Group has adopted a multi-segment strategy in order to serve a variety of the segments in the hospitality industry, reflecting the trends in this sector towards full service convention-led hotels, the growth in budget hotels and the ongoing development of suite-hotels and deluxe resorts.

InterContinental Hotels Group's marketers have considered a host of customer characteristics, requirements and behaviours in developing the company's brands and their respective brand positionings. These

FIGURE 17.5   InterContinental Hotels Group: Key Brands

InterContinental Hotels and Resorts	InterContinental was the first truly international hotel brand in the world, and quickly became the symbol of glamour, sophistication and success that years later, continue to define global travel. The brand is committed to providing its guests with memorable and unique experiences that enrich their lives and broaden their outlook. InterContinental offers services and amenities specifically designed for the international business traveller, while maintaining the delicate balance of luxury expectations with authentic local experiences that enhance the leisure stay as well. Located in more than 60 countries, InterContinental continues to expand in key destinations around the globe. www.intercontinental.com
Crowne Plaza Hotels and Resorts	Crowne Plaza Hotels and Resorts is *The Place to Meet*. The ideal upscale hotel choice for small-to-medium-sized business meetings, Crowne Plaza provides personalized service and one point of contact for hassle-free, successful meetings. In addition to superior meetings offerings, Crowne Plaza recognizes the importance of getting a great night's sleep while travelling and now guests can enjoy the brand's *Sleep Advantage* programme including a sleep kit (complete with ear plugs and eye mask), quiet zones, guaranteed wake-up calls and new bedding. As always, Crowne Plaza hotels provide quality fitness facilities, upscale dining and exceptional room accommodation. Crowne Plaza hotels are located in major city, resort and airport destinations worldwide www.crowneplaza.com
Hotel Indigo	Hotel Indigo is the industry's first branded lifestyle boutique hotel experience. It is uniquely designed to appeal to style savvy guests who desire affordable luxury, genuine service and an alternative to traditional "beige" hotels without sacrificing any of the business amenities they have come to expect. Renewal is the soul of Hotel Indigo's retail-inspired design concept – thoughtful changes that are made throughout the year to keep the hotel fresh, similar to the way retailers change their window displays. Guestrooms feature signature murals, area rugs, fluffy duvets and slip covers that will change periodically, while public spaces will be transformed seasonally through changing aromas, music, artwork, murals and directional signage. From relaxed café dining to high-style rooms – Hotel Indigo creates an intriguing, warm and inviting environment for guests. www.hotelindigo.com
Holiday Inn Hotels, Resorts and Sub-brands	As the most recognized lodging brand in the world, Holiday Inn Hotels and Resorts continues to welcome more guests every year than any other hotel brand. Holiday Inn Hotels provide the services that business travellers need, while also offering a comfortable atmosphere where guests can relax and enjoy amenities such as restaurants and room service, swimming pools, fitness centres and comfortable lounges. The casual atmosphere and amenities such as meeting and on-site business facilities, *KidSuites* rooms, *Kids Eat Free* and *Kids Stay Free* programmes, *Holidome Indoor Recreation Centres* and *Indoor Waterparks* demonstrate the long-standing commitment of Holiday Inn Hotels and Resorts to serving travellers and have helped to establish the brand as "America's Favourite Hotel". www.holidayinn.com

Holiday Inn Select is the hotel partner for individuals with a passion for business and an appreciation for value. Located throughout North and South America near business centres and airports, Holiday Inn Select hotels feature business class rooms, 24-hour business services, comprehensive meeting facilities and services.

Holiday Inn SunSpree Resorts: whether travelling to a tropical escape or a mountain getaway, we make it easy for the entire family to have fun together! Our casual atmosphere and modern facilities offer all of the conveniences you're looking for, like a great restaurant, in-room refrigerator, laundry facility, expansive pool area, and a variety of recreational facilities. Our friendly staff and trained *Activities' Coordinators* schedule numerous adult events and supervise children's activities as well.

Located in Europe and South Africa, each Holiday Inn Garden Court hotel has a style and character unique to its location. The Holiday Inn Garden Court hotels offer quality guest rooms, meeting and leisure facilities, as well as a number of other services and amenities.

Nickelodeon Family Suites by Holiday Inn. Nickelodeon, the number-one kids' brand, and Holiday Inn Hotels and Resorts partner to bring Nick's brand philosophy of putting kids first in everything it does into all aspects of the Nick Hotels. The hotels feature the popular Nickelodeon signature entertainment and style in a family-friendly, all-suite, resort atmosphere. Two- and three-bedroom themed *KidSuites*, *Daily Nicktoon Character Breakfast*, *Kids Eat Free* programme, *Waterpark* pools and nightly scheduled Nick shows are among the unique amenities of these one of a kind kid-focused resorts.

Holiday Inn Express continues to set the pace in the mid-scale without food and beverage hotel category as the fastest-growing brand, opening on average two new hotels every week. Holiday Inn Express invites guests to *Stay Smart* by offering travellers competitive rates and convenient locations around the globe. All hotels offer the *Express Start* breakfast bar, which features traditional morning favourites, as well as *Smart Roast* 100% Arabica coffee and warm cinnamon rolls made with an exclusive recipe developed especially for Holiday Inn Express. Guests will also experience the new *SimplySmart* shower which delivers a clean, simple and more functional bathing experience. It features an exclusive multi-function showerhead by Kohler® designed to compensate for all sorts of water pressure challenges. Guests will enjoy the *SimplySmart* bedding collection where guests will find new crisp fresh bedding which features an attractive decorative top sheet, a medium-weight duvet blanket and soft 200 thread-count sheets. *Simply Smart* bedding is currently being implemented at Holiday Inn Express hotels across North America. Now, that's smart!
www.hiexpress.com

Staybridge Suites   An innovative all-suite hotel meeting the needs of extended-stay guests. It's ideal for travellers seeking a residential-style hotel that's perfect for business, relocation and vacations. Whether it's a studio, one-bedroom or two-bedroom/two-bath suite, guests will find everything they need to make it their place. Each suite comes with a fully-equipped kitchen and separate living and work areas. Guests also enjoy free high-speed Internet access, a complimentary breakfast buffet, *Sundowner* evening receptions and 24-hour business services.
www.staybridge.com

Candlewood Suites	Candlewood Suites is focused on comfort, space and value for extended-stay guests. At more than 112 newly constructed Candlewood Suites hotels throughout North America guests find spacious studio and one-bedroom suites, each with its own fully equipped kitchen, executive desk, VCR and CD players, recliners and two-line telephones with voice mail. The fitness centre and complimentary guest laundry are open around the clock, and guests can take advantage of the 24-hour *Candlewood Cupboard*, where they will find snacks, refreshments, entrées and necessities available on the honour system. Candlewood Suites hotels offer guests all of this at a very comfortable price. www.candlewoodsuites.com

include the duration of stay, hotel location and proximity to other addresses, amenities and services sought or expected, desired luxury, value-for-money, hotel ambience and 'feel', hotel usage, size of guest room, purpose of stay, usage characteristics and customer profiles, amongst other variables. As a result, the company operates a large portfolio of hotel and resort brands. The key brands are summarized in the table, using the company's own descriptions of its brands' positionings.

The mix of brands and the selection of target market segments evident in Figure 17.5 have brought significant growth to InterContinental Hotels, allowing the group to demonstrate shareholder value and address market developments. There are some interesting marketing planning implications for this case.

The options for undertaking marketing planning in this complex and global organization include:

1 A centralized head office developed top-level marketing plan, based on macro hospitality industry drivers and corporate objectives.

This approach to marketing planning would be the most straightforward and cost effective to operationalize. However, there would be little added value to marketers handling an individual brand's marketing activities in a local market, and probable frustration with these marketers thinking that the resulting plans had little relevance to their challenges.

2 Regionalized marketing planning, to reflect varying situations around the world regarding consumer expectations, competition, marketing environment forces and the company's respective capabilities in each territory.

Market dynamics vary considerably around the world, so a 'one solution fits all' approach to marketing planning is unlikely to bring many benefits. However, the company cannot resource implementing dozens of different marketing plans, so a compromise would be required. One global marketing plan would not provide adequate direction or regional flexibility to address market challenges, but if individual hotel brands in each national market create a plan, there would be significant difficulty in operationalizing so many plans.

3 Sector-led or segment level marketing planning, so that the up-market brands' plans are produced together, the budget sector brands' plans are created as a set, with plans for suite-hotel brands and resorts also produced in a coordinated manner.

There is much to be said for sharing the burden of marketing analyses and strategizing between brands operating in the same markets and with similar brand positionings. In order to maintain distinctive brand positionings and execute effectively the brands' target market strategies, the execution of marketing strategies should not be too rigidly harmonized across brands. For example, were InterContinental and Crowne Plaza to become identical in terms of marketing mixes and brand positionings, there would be no benefits from operating as separate brands. Currently, they are able to tailor their propositions to cater for different usage behaviours.

4 Brand-led marketing planning, enabling each separate hotel brand to operate as standalone business units, producing their own marketing plans.

The separate hotel brand management teams are inevitably focused on their own brand and would prefer to develop marketing plans that support their performance targets and market positioning. However, there is the danger that there would be too much of a proliferation of localized planning with much duplication of activities during the marketing planning processes adopted by the separate brand teams.

The marketing planning challenge

The challenge is to undertake marketing planning in a way that creates economies of effort and fosters the sharing of marketing intelligence, while providing marketing managers and management teams with sufficient focus and flexibility to properly support their brand and its regional operations to address their market challenges.

This situation is not unique to either InterContinental Hotels Group or to the hospitality industry. Many organizations in other markets have to agree the remit and scope of their marketing planning activity, striving for a balance between localized detail and relevance versus the cost, complexity and efficiency of the marketing planning activity and the subsequent roll-out of the resulting marketing plans.

When too localized an approach is adopted, there are implementation burdens and many duplications of activity, but marketing plans focused on addressing specific market challenges will result. If overly centralized, the marketing planning is quicker, cheaper and less complicated, but the resulting plans lack detailed direction for addressing local problems and maximizing opportunities.

QUESTIONS FOR DISCUSSION

1 A brand-led approach to marketing planning is favoured by many global organizations, treating each brand as a business unit responsible for undertaking marketing planning. What are the advantages and disadvantages of this approach?

2 In order to opt for a centralized head-office-based approach to marketing planning, what would InterContinental Hotels Group need to do in order to ensure regional market dynamics steer the resulting marketing strategy and plan?

3 Assuming InterContinental Hotels Group prefers to permit each separate brand's leadership team to produce its own marketing plan, what steps should be taken to share market insights and learnings across the company's many brands and management teams?

4 As the Marketing Director for Holiday Inn Express, what aspects of the *ASP* process to marketing planning would be most important and why?

APPENDIX

In order to develop a robust marketing plan, it is necessary to undertake the core analyses as described in Part Two, update the target market strategy accordingly and then specify appropriate marketing programmes to take to market. This section of *Marketing Planning* brings together these 'must do' stages of effective marketing planning, leading to the plan's recommendations to be implemented. By sequentially addressing these templates, a rigorous process will be followed and a well-specified marketing plan will result.

APPENDIX FIGURE 2.1 Summary of existing target markets/segments

Existing customer group, target market or market segment label	These customer's key needs (KCVs)	Adopted descriptions used by the organization to describe the target market/ market segment
1		
2		
3		
4		
5		
6		
7		
8		

- Rank target markets/market segments in column 1 in order of importance (performance) to the organization
- For each market/customer group/market segment, rank the KCVs listed in column 2 in order of importance to these business customers or consumers
- Define the key customer value (KCV) term if required so as to avoid any ambiguity

APPENDIX FIGURE 2.2   Changing importance of priority markets

Rank order of markets by year										
Target market or segment	1999	2000	2001	2002	2003	2004	2005	2006	2007	2008
1										
2										
3										
4										
5										
6										
7										
8										

Reasons for major changes

- Rank each market's/segment's importance over the years. Importance may be in terms of sales volumes, market share, profitability or contributions
- Explain any major changes in rank position year on year

APPENDIX FIGURE 2.4   The ABC sales: contribution proforma

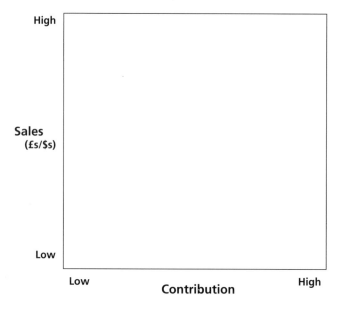

> • **Locate each market, market segment, or principal customer on the sales: contribution chart.**

APPENDIX FIGURE 3.1   Core market trends and predictions

Year	Sales volumes (units)	Sales £s/$s	Market size	Business's market share	Number of customers	Number of main competitors
2002						
2003						
2004						
2005						
2006						
2007						
2008						
2009						
2010						
2011						

- Complete as many columns as possible
- Information for 2008 (current year) onwards is based on predictions
- For many markets, the organization will not know market shares
- Principal customers: most businesses have an "80:20" split – the bulk of sales (e.g.: "80%") comes from a minority of customers (e.g.: "20%")
- Principal competitors (direct) indicate the level of market activity and to a degree, the "attractiveness" of the market

APPENDIX FIGURE 3.2   The marketing environment issues

Summary of core issues

Macro environment
(legal, regulatory and political, societal, technological, economic)

Micro environment
(direct and substitute competition, new entrants, supplier influence, customer buying power)

Principal implications to the organization of these issues

- Consider the wide range of potentially relevant aspects
- Be prudent and objective – list only important concerns
- List the most pressing/crucial issues first
- Have evidence to support these assertions
- Have facts with sources with which to defend statements

APPENDIX FIGURE 4.2 The SWOT analysis

Strengths	Weaknesses

Opportunities	Threats

- Rank (list) points in order of importance
- Only include key points/issues
- Have evidence to support these points or exclude them
- Strengths and Weaknesses should be relative to main competitors
- Strengths and Weaknesses are *internal* issues
- Opportunities and Threats are *external* marketing environment issues

What are the core implications from these issues?

APPENDIX FIGURE 5.3   Customers, KCVs, buying process steps and core influences – the buying proforma

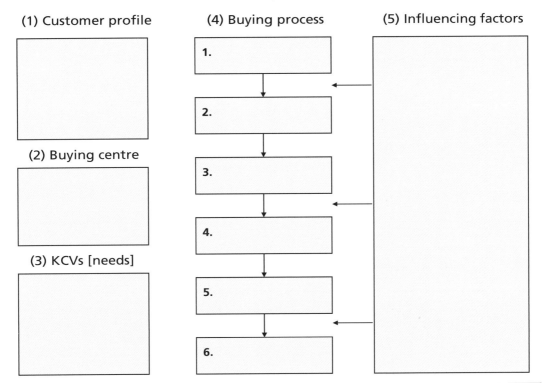

- Record the buying process, influences on each stage, typical customer profile and KCVs for each customer group or market segment. Start in the left-hand column and work across left-to-right
- Number the *Influences* and indicate on the arrows which *Influences* apply to each separate step in the *Buying Process*
- Note: the KCVs should match Figure 2.1 and be listed in order of importance to the customer
- A worked example appears on p. 43

© Sally Dibb & Lyndon Simkin

APPENDIX FIGURE 6.2   Competitive positions and differential advantage proforma

		Market/segment 1	Market/segment 2
Market leader	ID: Market share: KCVs: Weaknesses: Differential adv:		
Challenger 1	ID: Market share: KCVs: Weaknesses: Differential adv:		
Challenger 2	ID: Market share: KCVs: Weaknesses: Differential adv:		
Challenger 3	ID: Market share: KCVs: Weaknesses: Differential adv:		
Follower 'Me Too'	ID: Market share: KCVs: Weaknesses: Differential adv:		
Fast mover	ID: Market share: KCVs: Weaknesses: Differential adv:		
Nicher	ID: Market share: KCVs: Weaknesses: Differential adv:		

- Record the competitive positions separately for each target market/segment, using a column for each
- The KCVs on this chart are those KCVs that each competitor is able to match/serve
- Most companies do not have a DA (differential advantage), so this slot may be left blank for many companies' positions
- If competitors' market shares are known, enter them in the column. Often such data are not known. There is *no* need to list actual %s for market share changes, current year versus last year. Key to market share entries: ++ large market share increase; + small market share increase; − small market share decline; − − large market share decline
- There should be as many columns as the company's markets or segments
- There is only one market leader, but probably many of each of the other competitive positions

© Sally Dibb & Lyndon Simkin

APPENDIX FIGURE 7.3   Information required for the DPM analysis

Market attractiveness			
Variables	Weightings	Scores	Ranking/totals

Business strength/Competitive position			
Variables	Weightings	Scores	Ranking/totals

- Select the variables felt to be most important. Complete the columns
- This information now needs to be plotted on a graph, Figure 7.4, as in Figure 7.1

What are the Implications from this analysis?

APPENDIX FIGURE 7.4 The DPM proforma

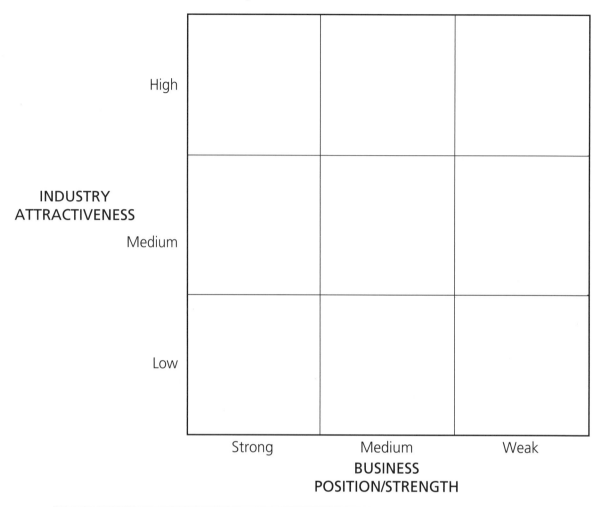

- First plot out the information recorded in Figure 7.3
- What are the implications from the resulting picture? Refer to Figure 7.2 on page 62 for guidance

APPENDIX FIGURE 7.6 The stages of the PLC

Segment and product	PLC stage	Implications

- For each product in each segment indicate the stage in the PLC reached – in column 2
- In column 3, suggest the more obvious strategic implications for each product

APPENDIX FIGURE 8.2 Determination of target markets

Market segment name (in order of priority)	Characteristics of market	Opportunity: why chosen as a target priority	Existing product/ sevice offered

- List target markets in order of importance (rank)
- State why each market is important
- Summarize the products offered to each market

APPENDIX FIGURE 8.3   Identification of Differential Advantages (DAs)

Segment name	Identified advantages (strengths) for the business over rivals	Are advantages sufficient basis for a differential advantage?
1		
2		
3		
4		
5		
6		
7		
8		

- Record any DAs held by the organization over rivals
- Remember a strength is only a possible DA if target customers desire it and rivals do not offer it
- Consider that to be sufficient for a DA, the strength must be cost effective and in the short term, defensible

APPENDIX FIGURE 8.5   The Positioning map

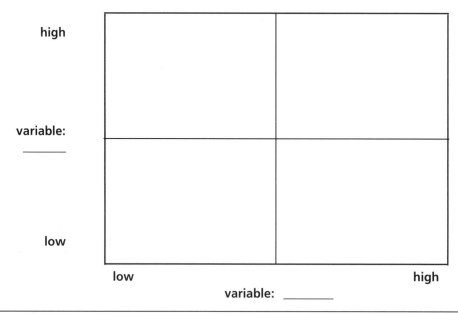

- Let customer feedback specify the KCVs to use on the map's axes
- Plot customers' perceptions of the relative positionings (locations) on the map of the organization's and leading competitors' brands or products
- Consider where ideally the organization's products or brands should be positioned.

APPENDIX FIGURE 9.1   Marketing strategy summary statement

Emerging opportunity to pursue + existing opportunities to support	Principal reasons	Key target markets or market segments

Core targeted segments/markets						
Segment	1:	2:	3:	4:	5:	6:
Principal reason for segment being targeting priority						
Likely sales Current year (units) Likely sales next year						
KCVs per segment						
Required brand positioning						
Main two competitors						
Principal competitive threat						
Differential advantage (DA)						
Key problems to overcome						
Capital implications from strategy						

- **This is the overall statement of marketing strategy and must be fully completed**

APPENDIX FIGURE 10.1 Marketing objectives

General strategic marketing objectives	
• • • • • •	
Segment:	Objective:
Segment:	Objective:
Segment:	Objective:
Segment:	Objective:
Segment:	Objective:
Segment:	Objective:
• First list overall marketing strategy objectives • Indicate the most important differences for leading target markets • Include a time scale for each objective	

APPENDIX FIGURE 10.2 The gap chart

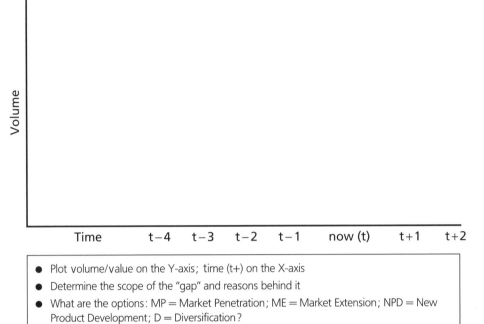

- Plot volume/value on the Y-axis; time (t+) on the X-axis
- Determine the scope of the "gap" and reasons behind it
- What are the options: MP = Market Penetration; ME = Market Extension; NPD = New Product Development; D = Diversification?
- -:-:- = Projected Volume; ——— = desired Volume

APPENDIX FIGURE 11.1 Summary by target market of KCVs and DAs

	Target market or segment 1	Target market or segment 2	Target market or segment 3	Target market or segment 4	Target market or segment 5	Target market or segment 6
Summary of KCVs						
Main competitive threat to the company						
Any company DA? Which strengths to leverage?						
Desired product or brand positioning?						

APPENDIX FIGURE 11.2 Customer perceptions – the organization versus leading rivals

Current perceptions – segment: _____				
Positive		Neutral	Negative	
++	**+**	**+/−**	**−**	**−−**
Brand awareness				
Product awareness				
Product/brand image				
Quality of product/ deliverable				
After sales Liaison/support				
Value of product/ deliverable				
Product performance				
On-time delivery				
Service professionalism				
Technical expertise				
Other:				
Other:				
Other:				

NB: Competitor 1 is: Competitor 2 is:

- Produce one proforma per targeted segment
- First enter the organization's own rating: ++, +, +/−, − or − −. NB: ++ = very positive/good;
  +/− = neutral; − − − = highly negative/very poor
- Second enter the ratings for the two leading rivals in the segment
- Use this coding to mark companies on the chart: 0 = the organization; 1 = main rival;
  2 = second main rival. Name these competitors on the proforma

In the context of these perceptions and the standing versus leading rivals, on which features must the organization immediately focus?

APPENDIX FIGURE 11.3   Summary of required product/service mix

Target market or segment	Title of the organization's relevant product or service	Product or service description
1		
2		
3		
4		

- List out existing products/services pertinent to each target market's or segment's needs and KCVs
- Column 2 = popular name/acronym; column 3 = "lay person's" description

Segment/market	Additional product/service requirements	Product/service attributes	Why required

- In this section, detail any new/additional products needed in the light of the marketing analyses to maintain the organization's competitive position, facilitate the organization's target market strategy or address identified opportunities
- Note, the "new product" could be a hybrid of activities which cuts across the organization's divisions/departments/sectors

APPENDIX FIGURE 11.4 Required service levels to support the product mix

	Segment 1	Segment 2	Segment 3	Segment 4
People				
Advice/guidance				
Ongoing support				
Facilities				
Other:				
Other:				
Training requirements				
Resource implications				

- This Figure requests information concerning service aspects of the product offer. The products *per se* (their tangible attributes) are detailed in Figure 11.3
- Some service aspects will require retraining/orientation of personnel interfacing with customers
- These "soft" issues connected with the product offering – such as warranties, technical advice, consumer finance, parts availability, etc – will require resourcing

APPENDIX FIGURE 11.5   Summary of current advertising and promotion

Nature of campaign What was done, when, which promotional mix elements
Campaign objectives For example, create brand awareness; generate sales leads; counteract rival's campaign; support new product   launch; etc
Cost of programme (if known)
Results of programme (if known)
• Complete a proforma per targeted segment • Note: the promotional mix includes advertising, publicity and public relations, sales promotion, personal selling,   sponsorship, direct mail and literature, as well as the internet and direct communications – all forms of promotional activity

APPENDIX FIGURE 11.6   Key promotional activity required

Promotional task	Targeted markets or segments							
	1	2	3	4	5	6	7	8
Build brand awareness								
Build brand image								
Build product awareness								
Build product image								
Position against competitors								
Re-position against competitors								
Create primary demand for product								
Induce trial								
Influence customers' KCVs								
Generate sales leads								
Promote after sales liaison								
Influence customer buying process								
Nurture ongoing relationship								
Promote collaboration								
Promote within the organization								
Other:								
Other:								
Other:								

- Indicate promotional requirements per targeted segment
- Keep selections to the bare minimum – too many will not be feasible or cost effective. If most boxes are ticked, revisit the list to prioritize

APPENDIX FIGURE 11.7   Desired promotional programmes

Promotion objectives (priorities)
Suggested advertising and promotions programmes Including likely tools/techniques
Anticipated budget required
Timing and scheduling of promotional activity
Agency/supplier
● Complete a proforma per targeted segment/market

APPENDIX FIGURE 11.8   Summary of marketing channel requirements

NB: If no dealers/distributors are involved in sales transactions, ignore this proforma!

Target market/segment: _____ Requirement:
Target market/segment: _____ Requirement:
Target market/segment: _____ Requirement:
Target market/segment: _____ Requirement:
Overall policy changes:
Personnel and service improvements required:
● State required dealer and distribution changes necessary to facilitate the target market strategy and associated marketing programmes (a) per core segment, (b) overall in the territory/market

APPENDIX FIGURE 11.9   Sales links through suppliers/contractors/partners

NB: This is relevant to organizations enjoying direct relationships with customers

Market/segment:_____
Nature of links with suppliers/contractors/consortium partners
Scope for the organization to use links for sales leads
Requirements to enable the organization to use these links
● Existing links/working relationships with third parties or intermediaries such as suppliers, contractors, consortium partners may form the basis for generating sales leads if handled with such an aim

APPENDIX FIGURE 11.10 Summary of pricing policy changes

	The organization			Principal competitor:_____			
Target market or market segment	Achieved price (A)	Desired price or bid price (D)	A−D(+/−) and reason for discrepancy	Product name	Achieved price (A)	Desired price (D)	A−D (+/−)

Summary of required pricing changes and pricing/bid policy alterations

- Inevitably the analyses will have revealed the need to modify pricing. The stated strategy will also require changes to pricing policies
- If information is known about the leading competitor, include it. Identify this competitor
- If bid problems are relevant and known/realized, explain in the lower section of box

In the light of the marketing analyses, are there any pricing policy changes required?

Of current pricing/bid arrangements, what aspects are worthy of development? What features are causing problems?

APPENDIX FIGURE 11.11 Process/customer liaison improvements required

Area requiring attention	Explanation/definition	Required action
Market information		
Product information		
Flows of information for bids/pricing		
Demonstrations		
Handling enquiries		
Pre-delivery advice		
Commercial support to customers		
Technical support		
Back-up advice		
Payment conditions/customer credit		
Inter-personnel relationships		
Communication with clients		
Handling visits		
Communication with suppliers		
Feedback to clients/suppliers		
Training		
Other:		
Other:		

- This is the organization helping customers; making life easier for customers to deal with the organization; improving flows of information and communications

APPENDIX FIGURE 12.1 Summary of programme tasks, timing and costs

Programme or marketing mix task	Person or department responsible	Date(s) for activity	Anticipated cost	Implications for the organization

- The main marketing mix requirements from Chapter 11 should be entered in column 1
- People must now take "ownership" of the identified actions in Chapter 11 and determine schedules and programme costs

APPENDIX FIGURE 12.2   Summary of responsibilities

Person or department	Responsibility/ task	Dates/ timings	External supplier/ agency

- Allocate the tasks detailed in Figure 12.1 to individual managers or departments
- Specify when these activities must take place

APPENDIX FIGURE 12.3   Summary of costs and budget implications

Task	Cost	Any budget implications for the organization?

- Summarize the costs/budgets for each of the marketing programme activities detailed in Chapter 11
- Outline any implications from the combined totals of these costs

APPENDIX FIGURE 13.1　Summary of anticipated knock-on impacts

Area of impact	Implication/required action/by whom

- Detail the likely knock-on impacts
- Consider the action required to facilitate the plan's unhindered implementation

APPENDIX FIGURE 13.2　Ongoing marketing research requirements

Information gap	Likely research activity	Timing	Cost

- Specify required marketing research activity

APPENDIX FIGURE 13.3 Medium-term work required

Area	Required work
Internal structuring/operations	
Market development	
Resource base	
Products and product mix	
Sales force and customer service	
Marketing channels	
Promotional activity/evaluation	
Pricing and payment terms	
Training	
Recruitment	
Other:	
● Specify the longer term marketing requirements	

APPENDIX FIGURE 13.4 Monitoring the performance

Monitored issue	Expected result (6 mths)	Actual outcome (6 mths)	Reason for gap	Expected result (12 mths)	Actual outcome (12 mths)	Reason for gap

- Determine measures for benchmarking progress
- Expected results should include sales, contributions, attitudinal data relating to customers' perceptions of brand positioning and their views on customer satisfaction

APPENDIX FIGURE 14.1 The marketing planning progress audit

Progress in addressing market challenges			
Key identified threats	Agreed actions in the plan	Progress status	Remedial recommendations
Key identified opportunities	Agreed actions in the Plan	Progress status	Remedial recommendations
Essential weaknesses to fix	Agreed actions in the plan	Progress status	Remedial recommendations

Progress in marketing strategy roll-out			
Target market strategy priorities	Agreed actions in the plan	Progress status	Remedial recommendations
Segment selection Key account list			
Brand positioning			
Basis for competing			
Product/service mix			
Customer engagement/handling			
MarComms			
Pricing			
Channel issues			
Partner/supplier issues			

Progress in marketing programme roll-out				
Agreed action	Whose task	Scheduled date	Current status of action	Recommendation

Performance assessment			
Stated performance expectation	Current performance	Nature of any gap	Recommendations

Addressing under-performance		
Under-performance issues	*Reasons identified*	*Recommendations*
Operations		
Marketing		
Delivery to the customer		
Others		

Capability and resource deficiencies to fix	
Gaps and deficiencies in capabilities	*Recommendations*
Resourcing problems	*Recommendations*

Market dynamics and emerging challenges	
Key challenges in the market	*Recommendations*
Competitor reaction/activities	
Customer response/requirements	
Marketing environment forces	
Supply chain issues	

BIBLIOGRAPHY

Dibb, S. and L. Simkin (1996) *The Marketing Planning Workbook*, Thomson: London.

Dibb, S. and L. Simkin (2001) 'Overcoming Planning Barriers: Four Case Studies', *Industrial Marketing Management*, 30, 609–25.

Dibb, S. and L. Simkin (2008) *Market Segmentation Success: Making It Happen!*, Hawarth: New York.

Dibb, S., L. Simkin and D. Wilson (2008) 'Diagnosing and Treating Operational and Implementation Barriers in Synoptic Marketing Planning', *Industrial Marketing Management*, February.

Dibb, S., L. Simkin, O. C. Ferrell and W. Pride (2006) *Marketing: Concepts and Strategies*, Houghton Mifflin: Boston.

McDonald, M. (2007) *Marketing Plans: How to Prepare Them, How to Use Them*, Elsevier Butterworth Heinemann: Oxford.

Simkin, L. (2000) 'Delivering Effective Marketing Planning', *Targeting, Measurement and Analysis for Marketing*, 8(4), 335–50.

Simkin, L. (2002) 'Tackling Implementation Impediments to Marketing Planning', *Marketing Intelligence & Planning*, 20(2), 120–6.

Simkin, L. (2002) 'Barriers Impeding Effective Implementation of Marketing Plans – a New Research and Training Agenda', *Journal of Business and Industrial Marketing*, 17(1), 8–22.

Porter, M. (1979) 'How Competitive Forces Shape Strategy', *Harvard Business Review*, 47, 137–45.

Porter, M. (2004a) *Competitive Strategy*, The Free Press: New York.

Porter, M. (2004b) *Competitive Advantage*, The Free Press: New York.

INDEX